THE AMERICAN SONG BOOK

THE AMERICAN SONG BOOK

THE TIN PAN ALLEY ERA

Philip Furia and Laurie Patterson

OXFORD
UNIVERSITY PRESS

OXFORD
UNIVERSITY PRESS

Oxford University Press is a department of the University of Oxford. It furthers
the University's objective of excellence in research, scholarship, and education
by publishing worldwide. Oxford is a registered trade mark of Oxford University
Press in the UK and certain other countries.

Published in the United States of America by Oxford University Press
198 Madison Avenue, New York, NY 10016, United States of America

Library of Congress Cataloging-in-Publication Data
Furia, Philip, 1943–
The American song book / Philip Furia and Laurie Patterson.
volumes   cm
Includes bibliographical references.
Contents: Volume I. The Tin Pan Alley era—
ISBN 978-0-19-939187-5 (alk. paper)—Pbk: ISBN 978-0-19-939188-2 (alk. paper)
1. Popular music—United States—History and criticism.
I. Patterson, Laurie.   II. Title.
ML3477.F86   2016
782.421640973—dc23   2015010162

1 3 5 7 9 8 6 4 2
Printed in the United States of America
on acid-free paper

TO THE MEMORY OF SHELDON MEYER,

Senior Vice President, Editorial, Oxford University Press,

who did so much to keep these songs alive and kicking.

Acknowledgments

The authors want to thank Les Block, who has always supported their research on American popular song. Les, along with Jerry Osterberg, co-editor of the newsletter of the New York Sheet Music Society, steered us toward Sandy Marrone, also with the New York Sheet Music Society, who graciously provided us with original sheet music for most of the songs in this book. We also want to thank the UCLA Archive of Popular Music for providing copies of sheet music, particularly Peggy Alexander, Simon Elliot, Benjamin Formaker-Olivas, and Amy Wong for the assistance they provided.

Many of the anecdotes about songs were uncovered in research Philip Furia conducted with co-author Michael Lasser for their book, *America's Songs: The Stories Behind the Songs of Broadway, Hollywood, and Tin Pan Alley* (New York: Routledge, 2006). We are grateful to Michael for agreeing to let us draw upon that mutual research. Norman Hirschy, our editor at Oxford University Press, helped us plan this book, gave valuable advice along the way, and found excellent reviewers of the initial proposal as well as the completed manuscript.

We also want to thank WHQR, Wilmington, North Carolina's public radio station, which enabled Phil Furia, with producer George Scheibner, to create a daily radio program, *The Great American Song Book*. With his extensive and eclectic knowledge of music, George provided many insights into these songs. Our thanks extend to WHQR's station manager Cleve Callison and members of the station staff.

Phil Furia and Laurie Patterson also presented live versions of *The Great American Song Book* with numerous singers and musicians, including David Boeddinghaus, Frank Bongiorno, Philip Bruschi, Grenoldo Frazier, Banu Gibson, Jeff Hamilton, Jack Krupicka, Brad and Julie Moranz, Stephanie Nakasian, Hod O'Brien, Julie Rehder, Susan Reeves, Nina Repeta, John Sheridan, James Singleton, Prince Taylor, and Sara Westermark. Working with such talented and knowledgeable performers has enhanced our understanding of these songs. We would also like to thank the departments of Computer Science and Art and Art History at the University of North Carolina Wilmington, especially Amy Kirschke, for providing needed technology.

Finally, we thank our daughter, Olivia Leona Patterson Furia, who had to put up with both her parents working on this book while also serving as chairs, respectively, of the Department of Computer Science and the Department of Theatre at the University of North Carolina Wilmington.

Contents

THE AMERICAN SONG BOOK

JEROME H. REMICK & COMPANY.

MUSIC PU

45 WHITNEY WARNER
DETROIT MUSIC NEW YORK

WHITNEY WAR
MUSIC

PRINTER

IPPER

PPER MUSIC PUBLISHERS.

LIPPER.

NEW YORK CLIPPER

JEROME H. REMICK & COMPANY

WILLIA

MORR

45
MUSIC
PUBLISHERS

MUSIC
PUBLISHERS

THOMAS YO

JEROME H. REMICK & COMPANY.
WHITNEY WARNER PUBLISHING CO

THOMAS YOUNG J

Introduction

THE SONGS THAT CONSTITUTE *The American Song Book* have done what popular songs are not supposed to do: *stayed* popular. The very notion of "popular" song, after all, depends upon transience: a song is popular for a period of time, then fades away, to be replaced by newer songs, remembered, if at all, by its original listeners as a "golden oldie." But hundreds of songs have not only endured but sound as fresh today as when they were first popular. We call them "standards" (the British, who love them as much as we do, call them "evergreens").

There are several reasons for the remarkable endurance of these songs. For one thing, they were written by *songwriters*. That may seem tautological, but in the 1920s, '30s, and '40s, songwriters usually did not perform their own songs as songwriters have increasingly done since the 1950s and '60s. Songwriters *wrote* songs, period. Singers *performed* songs. That specialization was further subdivided between composers, who wrote music, and lyricists, who set their melodies to words. Many of those composers, such as George Gershwin, Cole Porter, and Richard Rodgers, were classically trained and brought subtle sophistication to the simple musical formulas of popular song. They also wrote their songs on the piano—not, as composers have increasingly done in recent years, on the more musically limited guitar.

Lyricists such as Ira Gershwin, Lorenz Hart, and Dorothy Fields were schooled in the rigors of light verse. They wrote rondeaus and triolets, villanelles and ballades. They handled the intricacies of meter and rhyme with consummate skill (they would never, for example, rhyme "sometime" with "sunshine"). With wit and verve, they rang refreshing changes on the tired formulas of romantic love.

Most of the songs in *The American Song Book* were written by a handful—two or three dozen—of composers and lyricists. Almost all of them grew up in New York City, immigrants or the children of Jewish immigrants, and some of them knew each other. Ira Gershwin and E. Y. "Yip" Harburg not only went to the same school but were seated near one another alphabetically. When they discovered that they shared a love of light verse, Yip told Ira that his favorite poet was William Schwenck Gilbert. Ira tactfully asked if he knew that many of Gilbert's "poems" were really song lyrics. "There's music to it?" Yip asked. Harburg, who lived in the wretched poverty of New York's Lower East Side, followed Ira back to his comparatively luxurious middle-class apartment. When Ira put a recording of *H.M.S. Pinafore* on the family Victrola, Harburg was stunned. "There were all the lines I knew by heart, put to music. I was dumbfounded, staggered."[1]

Harburg dated his aspiration to become a lyricist from that moment, but he would learn that in American song, writing lyrics was a much more difficult undertaking than it was for Gilbert. In answer to that perennial question, "Which comes first, the music or the words?" with Gilbert and Sullivan, it was the words. Gilbert would essentially write a light-verse poem then Sullivan would set it to music. In American songwriting, it was the reverse: the composer would complete a melody, then the lyricist would set syllable to note, verbal phrase to musical phrase. It was like working a musical crossword puzzle. That Harburg, Ira Gershwin, and other American lyricists could rival Gilbert in witty rhymes and clever imagery is all the more amazing given that they were writing *to* music.

As professional songwriters working in New York and Hollywood, these composers and lyricists socialized with each other, and wherever they gathered, they demonstrated their latest efforts to one another. A composer wouldn't dare to play a bad chord with Jerome Kern sitting across the room; a lyricist would never use an off-rhyme with Larry Hart at his shoulder. While they were writing for a popular audience, they were also writing for each other.

Yet quality alone does not ensure longevity. Other factors had to be in alignment to help preserve these songs. To begin with, many of them were originally written for Broadway musicals. As these musicals were regularly revived in professional and amateur productions, the songs became familiar to an increasingly larger audience. Many, too, were written for Hollywood films—not just musical films but dramatic ones as well. We continue to enjoy these films, particularly those featuring Fred Astaire and Ginger Rogers, Judy Garland and Gene Kelly, and we relish the songs of Irving Berlin, Cole Porter, the Gershwins, and other songwriters who wrote as brilliantly for the screen as they did for the stage.

Beginning in the 1920s, jazz musicians found these songs, particularly their chord progressions, more engaging than the simple harmonies of traditional blues. Songs such as "I Got Rhythm" and "Body and Soul" have inspired countless improvisations by the greatest musicians, from Charlie Parker to Dizzy Gillespie, and *The American Song Book* has become the bedrock of the jazz repertory.

But what was the catalyst that transformed these great songs into enduring standards?

Enter Frank Sinatra.

While singers such as Lee Wiley and musicians such as Artie Shaw occasionally recorded older songs, no singer before Sinatra concentrated more on recording songs that were ten, twenty, even thirty years old. Sinatra had been the idol of bobby-soxers in the 1930s and '40s, but by the early '50s he was pushing forty. He was let go from Columbia Records when he refused to record songs he considered "crap," and his career went into decline.

Capitol, however, took a chance on Sinatra and paired him with the arranger Nelson Riddle. Beginning with *Songs for Young Lovers* in 1953, Sinatra made a series of albums on the new LP (Long-playing) discs. LPs were initially used for classical music, since a single disc could hold an entire symphony. Then LPs expanded to include original Broadway cast recordings and movie soundtracks. At Capitol, Sinatra expanded the LP repertoire even further by recording older songs, mostly from Broadway musicals. As "show tunes," these songs had more cachet than current pop songs, and Sinatra's albums helped establish them as "standards"—at the very moment popular music was being taken over by rock 'n' roll, epitomized by Elvis Presley.

If Sinatra helped preserve these songs, they, in turn, did a lot for him—as they have also done for aging rockers, such as Rod Stewart, who continue to record them under the aegis of *The Great American Song Book*. As songs written for Broadway musicals, these songs had what Ira Gershwin dubbed "particularity"—they were written for a particular character in a particular dramatic situation. As such, the persona created by the lyric is usually a more emotionally complex character than the "I" who sings to "you" in most run-of-the-mill pop songs. Indeed, Ira Gershwin did not consider himself a writer of "popular songs." All of his songs were written, as he put it, "to spec"—to fit a specific character in a specific situation. He even referred to the songs themselves as "lodgments"—tailored to fit a certain dramatic point in a show.

These "dramatic" songs played to Sinatra's skill as an actor (a skill recognized in 1953, when he received the Academy Award for Best Supporting Actor for his portrayal of Maggio in *From Here to Eternity*). Sinatra "became" the character delineated in the lyric, and in some of these songs, such as Johnny Mercer and Harold Arlen's "One for My Baby" ("It's quarter to three, there's no one in the place 'cept you and me, so set 'em up, Joe…") he acted out a miniature drama. With the new "high fidelity" recording equipment, Sinatra, who always claimed that his musical "instrument" was the microphone, could capture subtle nuances of emotion as he "read" a lyric.

What is striking about many of the songs Sinatra chose to record on his Capitol albums is that they were originally written for female performers. Women characters in Broadway musicals were often given a wider range of emotional shades—pensive, melancholy, vulnerable, tender—than male characters (who often were merely importunate). Of course, even though many of these songs were written for female characters in specific dramatic situations, songwriters always had their eye on the pop market and found ways that enabled a song to be rendered by both male and female singers. In some cases, ensuring maximum exposure for a song involved a complete overhaul of the lyric. In Rodgers and Hart's *Pal Joey*, "Bewitched" is sung by the hardened but horny character of Vera Simpson. A former stripper, she is now the mistress of a millionaire but nevertheless has an affair with "Joey" on the side and even installs him in his own nightclub. After one of their drunken romps, Vera wakes up surprisingly refreshed:

> *After one whole quart of brandy,*
> *Like a school girl I awake.*
> *With no Bromo Seltzer handy,*
> *I don't even shake.*

As she looks at her passed-out lover, she sings eight cynical choruses that range from worshipping the "trousers that cling to him," feeling "vexed again, perplexed again, Thank God I can be oversexed again," to getting over her lust and saying "finis" to "those ants in my pants." Little of this sensuality, however, appears in the lyric Hart wrote for the popular version of "Bewitched," which cleans up such lines as worshipping the "trousers that cling to him" to:

> *I'll sing to her (him)*
> *Each spring to her (him)*
> *And long or the day when I cling to her (him)*

It's this bowdlerized version of "Bewitched" that Sinatra—and most other singers—perform.

A more common way lyricists tailored a song for popularity beyond a show was to make only the verse of the song identify the singer as female but keep the all-important chorus androgynous. In "My Funny Valentine" (the first song in Sinatra's 1953 LP *Songs for Young Lovers*) from the Rodgers and Hart's 1937 musical *Babes in Arms*, the singer is in love with a guy named "Val" (short for "Valentine"). In the verse, she derides him as a homely, "dim-witted," and "slightly dopey gent." In the chorus, however, such mockery continues—"Your looks are laughable—unphotographable . . . Is your figure less than Greek? Is your mouth a little weak? When you open it to speak, are you smart?"—but are not identifiably feminine. While it is unusual for a man to list his beloved's faults before reassuring her "You're my fav'rite work of art," that odd twist is a refreshing change from the typical male's breathless praise of her every feature.

At a time when Sinatra was trying to redefine his singing persona apart from the bobby-soxer idol of the 1940s, the songs of Cole Porter, the Gershwins, and other Broadway songwriters gave him literate sophistication, wry tenderness, and wrenching vulnerability. Perhaps no song better illustrates how these "feminine" songs transformed Sinatra than "The Girl Next Door," the second song on his first album at Capitol. Originally written by Ralph Blane and Hugh Martin for Judy Garland in the movie *Meet Me in St. Louis* as "The Boy Next Door," the lyric voices a wistful longing befitting an adolescent girl, lamenting a neighbor who

Doesn't try to please me
Doesn't even tease me

In helping to make these songs standards that male as well as female vocalists could sing, Sinatra expanded *The American Song Book* with emotional intricacy and depth.

The success of Sinatra's Capitol albums prompted other singers, such as Tony Bennett, Doris Day, and Polly Bergen to follow suit. In 1956, Ella Fitzgerald began a series of "Song Book" albums at Verve with *Ella Fitzgerald Sings The Cole Porter Song Book.* Over the next ten years, in what Larry Stempel describes as a "conservative move at the time, given the rising tide of rock 'n' roll,"[2] Fitzgerald recorded albums dedicated to Rodgers and Hart, Duke Ellington, Irving Berlin, George Gershwin, Harold Arlen, Jerome Kern, and Johnny Mercer (the only one devoted exclusively to a lyricist).

In recent years, a new generation of singers—Linda Ronstadt (also with Nelson Riddle as her arranger), Willie Nelson (over the protests of his producer against his *Star Dust* album), Rod Stewart, Van Morrison, Carly Simon, the Supremes, Meat Loaf, Robert Palmer, K. D. Lang, Harry Connick Jr., Cher, Sting, Michael Bublé, Brian Wilson of the Beach Boys, Lady Gaga, and, recently, Paul McCartney—have paid their tributes to *The American Song Book*. In her liner notes to *Moonlight Serenade*, Carly Simon reverently writes, "I don't know if I've earned the right to sing these songs."

The most recent rocker to record an album of these songs is Bob Dylan, whose *Shadows in the Night* is a tribute to Frank Sinatra. "He never went away," Dylan has said. "All those things we thought were here to stay, they did go away. But he never did." The album includes Irving Berlin's "What'll I Do?" Rodgers and Hammerstein's "Some Enchanted Evening," and Johnny Mercer's English lyric to Joseph Kosma's melody for "Autumn Leaves." Like Willie Nelson, Rod Stewart, and other contemporary singers, Dylan renders these songs in his own distinctive style, which shows how durable they are. "There's nothing contrived in these songs," Dylan has said. "There's not one false word in any of them. They're eternal."[3]

In following Sinatra's lead by recording these standards, Dylan, McCartney, and other contemporary singers have made *The American Song Book* a wonderfully—and appropriately—*democratic* institution by voting, with their voices, for songs that constitute the closest thing we have to a body of classical music, which year after year, generation after generation, is reinterpreted by singers, musicians, and listeners.

Tin Pan Alley

———◆◆◆———

IT'S HARD TO BELIEVE that the musical gems in *The American Song Book* emerged from one of the most crassly commercial enterprises in American history—the sheet-music publishing industry known as "Tin Pan Alley." In 1900 the songwriter Monroe H. Rosenfeld, writing a story for the *New York Herald*, went to the stretch of West 28th Street between Broadway and Sixth Avenue where many of these publishers had their offices. There, out of the windows of the closely packed buildings, came the cacophony of dozens of upright pianos, creating, polishing, and demonstrating new songs. The racket, so the story goes, reminded Rosenfeld of rattling tin pans and inspired him to christen that section of 28th Street "Tin Pan Alley."

The location of Tin Pan Alley kept changing—it had started out in the 1880s around Union Square, then followed the movement of theaters uptown at the turn of the century, then migrated again in the 1920s to the stretch of Broadway between 42nd and 50th. By the 1960s, when sheet music had largely been displaced by records, Tin Pan Alley had shrunk to the confines of the Brill Building at 1619 Broadway, just above Times Square. Whatever its address, however, Tin Pan Alley was always located, as songwriters joked, "close to the nearest buck."

Commercial as it was, Tin Pan Alley's methods of producing and popularizing songs laid the groundwork for the masterpieces of Cole Porter, Rodgers and Hart, and the Gershwins. The very notion of "popularizing" a song was invented by these music publishers. Older, established publishers, such as Oliver Ditson & Co. of Boston, were not especially interested in publishing popular songs. Their main products were classical piano pieces, church hymnals, and music instruction booklets. Occasionally they might publish a song but only after it had already become popular through performances in minstrel or variety shows. Even then, demand for such songs was not heavy, since, as Warren Craig noted, "sheet music was found only in the nation's more affluent homes furnished with pianos."[1]

———◆◆◆———

In 1852, the sale of 75,000 copies of sheet music for Stephen Foster's "Massa's in de Cold, Cold Groun'" was considered phenomenal since music publishers did not try to promote songs. David Ewen observed of nineteenth-century music publishers:

> Composers, performers, even the public had to beat a path to their doors. To go out in search of song material, to manufacture songs for specific timely purposes or events, to find performers and even bribe them to introduce such songs, to devise ingenious strategy to get a public to buy the sheet music—all this was not in the philosophy of conducting a music-publishing venture.[2]

These techniques for producing and promoting popular songs would become the province of the sheet-music publishers of Tin Pan Alley.

The first song to become popular through a national advertising campaign was "Grandfather's Clock" in 1876, the same year the telephone was invented. By the end of the nineteenth century, mass production made pianos more affordable: the 1900 Montgomery Ward catalog advertised upright pianos for as little as one hundred dollars. As these pianos graced more and more middle-class parlors, home entertainment in the days before radio, record players, and television consisted of sing-alongs around the family piano. This created a demand for easily playable sheet music, and to meet that demand, a new kind of music publisher emerged in New York. For these publishers—Maurice Shapiro and Louis Bernstein, Leo Feist, Edwin Marks, Joseph Stern, the Witmark brothers—songs were *made* not *born*—"Made to Order" as one firm advertised its wares.

Most of these publishers were first- or second-generation Jewish immigrants who had swelled America's urban, commercial, and industrial expansion after the Civil War. Many of them had started out as salesmen. David Jasen writes that publishers "hired salesmen of clothing, notions and supplies to carry sample cases of music with them when they made their rounds throughout their territories."[3] Stern had sold neckties; Marks, notions and buttons; Feist had been field manager of the R and G Corset Company, figuring, as Kenneth Kanter said, "anyone who could sell corsets could also sell songs."[4]

And sell songs they did. What by the 1950s would be scandalously labeled "payola" began with these publishers as the perfectly acceptable practice of bribing vaudeville performers to sing their firm's songs. The bribe could range anywhere from offering a good cigar to giving a big-name performer such as Al Jolson a "cut in"—placing his name on the sheet music as one of the composers or lyricists of a song so that he would receive a portion of the royalties its sheet-music sales earned. The cost of sheet music could range from fifty to sixty cents, but the songwriters received only a few cents from each sale; the rest went to the publisher.

Even more effective in the promotion of songs was the practice of "plugging." In the publishing offices that lined 28th Street, piano "pluggers" relentlessly demonstrated their company's wares to vaudeville entertainers in search of new songs for their acts. Like human jukeboxes, pluggers also visited music stores where they demonstrated songs for the public in search of the latest hits. Since it was usually girls who were given piano lessons, many of the pluggers who worked in music stores were women. Setting up shop in the "dime store" chains that emerged after the founding of Woolworth's in 1879, they "sat at pianos all day, thumping out the latest songs for shoppers" and "turned the music department into the liveliest and busiest area of the stores."[5] Dime stores also brought the price of sheet music down to ten cents.

Male pluggers were sent out to restaurants, bars, anywhere crowds were gathered. They sometimes sat at a piano on the bed of a truck, serenading people on street corners, or from a balloon floating over Coney Island. The best place to plug a song, however, was in vaudeville. Vaudeville (a name that probably sprang from songs performed in theaters in the northern French region of Vau de Vivre—Valley of the Vivre River), emerged from Tony Pastor's theater in Union Square beginning in 1881. Pastor's theater diverged from the rowdy variety shows, aimed at male audiences in saloons, to "family acts" that women and children could enjoy.

By the end of the nineteenth century, vaudeville had displaced the minstrel show as the staple of musical theater. In minstrel shows, songs were performed with the entire company on stage, but in vaudeville songs were rendered by individual performers. Getting a vaudeville star to use your publishing company's latest song in her act gave it the biggest plug. One of the most innovative forms of plugging was the "singing stooge." A singer (often a young boy with a winning voice) would be planted in a theater audience. After a performer sang one of his company's new songs from the stage, the stooge would rise and, as if carried away by the song's beauty, sing an encore, inviting the audience to join in. It was as a singing stooge, at Tony Pastor's vaudeville theater, that Irving Berlin got his start on Tin Pan Alley.

After the turn of the century, vaudeville, following the example of the booking agency known as the Theatrical Syndicate, which sent shows to some seven hundred theaters across the country, expanded beyond New York into two huge national "circuits"—the "Keith-Albee" chain of theaters east of the Mississippi and the "Orpheum" circuit to the west of the river. As performers moved from theater to theater across the country, they gave new songs national exposure. Tin Pan Alley took advantage of these national networks by gracing sheet-music covers with photographs of vaudeville performers. With this array of plugging techniques, by 1910 most popular songs in America emerged from Tin Pan Alley.

Such mass marketing called for mass production, and the publishing houses of Tin Pan Alley also differed from traditional sheet-music publishers in that they produced the songs they sold rather than waiting for songwriters to come to them. The din that struck Monroe Rosenfeld's ear at Broadway and 28th Street came from the many cubicles where pianos were pounding out new songs assembly-line fashion. Publishers devised simple formulas for creating songs so that any new song would instantly sound familiar to the public because it was built along the same musical and lyrical lines of previous popular songs. These formulas were so simple that many successful "composers" could not read a note of music (including, for much of his career, Irving Berlin). They simply whistled or hummed a tune to one of the publishing house "arrangers," who would then transcribe, harmonize, and take it down in musical notation. Only then would a lyricist be called in to set words to the music. The theme and even the title of the lyric were usually dictated by the publisher, who kept his eye on the newspaper for topical subjects. One publisher read a newspaper story about a little girl who, soon after her mother had died, picked up the telephone and asked the "central" switchboard operator to connect her with heaven because that's where her mother was. The publisher immediately had his firm crank out "Hello, Central, Give Me Heaven."

In the 1880s and '90s, Tin Pan Alley songs followed the musical and lyrical formulas of nineteenth-century songs. That is, they were *strophic*—telling a story through a series of narrative verses ("In a cavern, in a canyon, excavating for a mine / Lived a miner forty-niner and his daughter Clementine.") and brief, repeated lyrical refrains of eight or sixteen bars ("Oh my darling, oh my darling, oh my darling Clementine / You are lost and gone forever…"). The music for the verses and the refrains was repeated, but while the lyrics for the verses recounted an unfolding story ("Light she was and like a fairy / And her shoes were number nine."), the lyrics for the refrains were as repetitive as the music ("Oh, my darling, oh, my darling…").

This traditional strophic formula was used by Tin Pan Alley songwriters to tell stories on a variety of subjects, from "The Pardon Came Too Late" through "The Picture That Is Turned to the Wall" to "The Convict and the Bird." Many of these songs were about romantic love, but love was nowhere near the preponderant subject it would become in popular songs in the 1920s, '30, and '40s. Still, the most phenomenally successful of these early Alley songs was about romantic misunderstanding, heartbreak, and remorse.

Charles K. Harris

———————◄◆◆◆►———————

CHARLES K. HARRIS'S "After the Ball" told the story—in three verses—of a little girl who crawls upon her uncle's knee and asks why he has never wed. The uncle then recounts the night "years ago" when he was at a ball with his fiancée. She asked him to fetch a glass of water, but when he returned he found her embracing another man. Shocked, he dropped the glass and stormed off, never to see her again. Years later, he learned that the man was her brother, and she was hugging him out of joy over her engagement. To top off this absurd misunderstanding, she died of a broken heart, and the uncle never married.

Harris wrote the song at the request of his tailor, who wanted a new song to sing in an amateur minstrel show. When Harris gave him "After the Ball," he said "I tried to impress upon him that this ballad contained three verses and that it was essential for him to sing them all, otherwise the effect of the simple story would be lost. He assured me that he would experience no trouble in that respect, as he had sung at a great many entertainments and never lost his nerve." On the night of the performance, the singer got through the first two verses, along with two renditions of the chorus, but at the third verse he forgot the words. "Deeply embarrassed, he was compelled to sit down without finishing the ballad. I immediately clutched my hat, silently stole out of the theater, and firmly resolved that never again shall an amateur singer introduce any new song of mine."[1]

The singer's lapse is understandable, since the lyric for the sixty-four bar verse is filled with arch diction ("list to the story"), verbal padding ("I'll tell it all"), awkward inversions ("Where she is now, pet, you will soon know"), and mismatches of musical and verbal accents (so that "**ball**room" has to be pronounced "ball**room**"). Harris, however, waved away such infelicities as the result of having to write lyrics to a completed melody. "Certain allowances should be made in order that the words may fit the music or rhythm, so as to give it that lilt or swing which makes for its popularity. When the song is rendered, these defects are not so apparent."[2]

Harris then tried to get May Howard of the Howard Burlesque Company to plug the song, but she balked at a line in the second verse, "Down fell the glass, pet, broken, that's all." "Miss Howard burst into laughter and said that if she ever attempted to sing that song in any burlesque theater where they drank beer, half the audience would drop their glasses on the floor just for the fun of it." She suggested that "if I eliminated the second verse containing the objectionable line, condensed my song to two verses and a chorus, she would sing it. I told Miss Howard that that one line was going to make the song a big hit."[3]

Undaunted, Harris kept trying to get singers to plug "After the Ball," and in 1892 he persuaded the prominent baritone J. Aldrich Libbey to sing it as part of his performance in *A Trip to Chinatown*, a popular stage show. As such, "After the Ball," was an "interpolation," a song added to a show after it had opened and which was not written by the composer of the show's original score.

> Libbey walked out to the footlights in full evening dress. The orchestra commenced playing the introduction to the song, and then Libbey, in his magnificent, clear, high barytone voice, sang the first verse and chorus. When he finished not a sound was heard. I was ready to sink through the floor. He then went through the second verse and the chorus, and again silence reigned. I was making ready to bolt…then came the third verse and chorus. For a full minute the audience remained quiet, and then broke loose with applause… The entire audience arose and, standing, wildly applauded for fully five minutes.

To Harris's delight, Libbey had rendered "After the Ball" with "overwhelming effect."[4]

Although Harris attributed much of that effect to his verse, it must have stemmed more from the chorus, for, as he also recalled at the performance, "Libbey was compelled to sing the chorus at least six times over."[5] Stilted and awkward as the verses are, the chorus is superb, both musically and lyrically. The lyric consists of a single sentence, beginning with four parallel phrases that match four rising musical phrases:

After the ball is over,
After the break of morn,
After the dancers' leaving,
After the stars are gone

As music and lyric rise to a climax, the off rhyme between "morn" and "gone" is barely noticeable, and the sentence reaches its main clause:

Many a heart is aching

But then the melody climbs even higher, traversing a full octave and even an interval beyond, and the lyric follows with a soaring subordinate clause:

If you could read them all;

As the music descends to its close, the lyric shifts from clause to phrase with what would become a staple Alley device for plugging a song—repeating its title at the conclusion so listeners would know what piece of sheet music to ask for at the music store.

Musically, Harris struck a balance between verse and chorus. Unlike most nineteenth-century songs, which have refrains of eight or sixteen measures, "After the Ball" has a chorus of thirty-two bars. As Charles Hamm has noted, by the end of the nineteenth century the relationship between verse and refrain had altered so that songs had fewer and fewer verses, and the "chief melodic material" had shifted to the refrain or, as it increasingly would be called, the "chorus."[6] One indication of that shift is that anyone who knows "After the Ball" today, either from its interpolation into the musical *Show Boat* or its use on the soundtrack of *Driving Miss Daisy*, can sing its chorus but not its verse.

"After the Ball" was Tin Pan Alley's first big national hit. It sold more than a million copies of sheet music—a staggering advance over Stephen Foster's sale of 75,000 copies of "Massa's in de Cold, Cold Groun'" some thirty years earlier. "After the Ball" caught the ear of John Philip Sousa, who had his band perform it at the Chicago World's Fair of 1893, which more than 27.5 million people visited, and over the next few years sheet-music sales topped five million copies. "After the Ball" proved that there was indeed money to be made on Tin Pan Alley.

After The Ball

As sung by

J. Aldrich Libbey

... The ...

Peerless Baritone in

HOYT'S

"A Trip to Chinatown"

BY

CHAS.

K. HARRIS,

... Author of ...

"KISS AND LET'S MAKE UP."

.. 5 ..

J. ALDRICH LIBBEY, the Peerless Baritone.

... Published by ....

CHAS. K. HARRIS,
MILWAUKEE, WIS.

After The Ball

CHAS. K. HARRIS

4

14

After The Ball 4

4

you   will   soon know._____   List   to   the   sto -
as   lov - ers   can._____   Down   fell   the   glass
the   let - ter   ran._____   That's   why   I'm   lone -

ry,   I'll   tell   it   all,_____   I   be-lieved   her
pet,   brok - en   that's   all,_____   Just   as   my
ly,   no   home   at   all,_____   I   broke   her

faith - less,   af - ter   the   ball.
heart___ was,   af - ter   the   ball.
heart___ pet,   af - ter   the   ball.

CHORUS

Af-ter the ball is o - ver,   Af-ter the break of morn,_____

After The Ball 4

16

After the dancers leaving, After the stars are gone; Many a heart is aching, if you could read them all; Many the hopes that have vanished After the ball.

After The Ball 4

No songwriter or music publisher epitomized the spirit of Tin Pan Alley—its enterprise, innovation, and "hustle"—more than Charles Kassell Harris. He was born into a large Jewish family in Poughkeepsie, New York; grew up in Saginaw, Michigan; then his family moved to Milwaukee when he was fourteen. Ever since childhood, he was fascinated by minstrel shows and especially by the banjo players. Unable to afford a banjo, he built a makeshift version out of a "flat tin oyster can and part of an old broom handle. I unwound the wire which held the broom together and, making some wooden keys, strung it up. In a rather crude way I was soon strumming a tune."[7] Soon he acquired a real banjo and taught himself to play proficiently.

In Milwaukee, he made money by giving banjo lessons and playing in local entertainments. After a while, "it seemed that the songs I had suggested at previous entertainments or minstrel shows had become monotonous to people. We were at a loss where we could procure new songs."[8] It was at this point that Harris began writing his own songs. When one of these met with mild success—but only earned him eighty-five cents in royalties—Harris realized that the money to be made in popular music went largely to the sheet-music publisher. He set up his own publishing company in Milwaukee then, after the success of "After the Ball," moved his firm to Union Square in New York, where other sheet-music publishers as well as theaters, saloons, dance halls, penny arcades, dime museums, and brothels were clustered.

One of his first innovations as a music publisher was to place photographs of singers on the covers of his sheet music. "I conceived the idea of placing photographs of prominent singers on the title pages of my songs.... The singer whose photograph appeared on the sheet music was thus the recipient of considerable free advertisement."[9] In turn, that advertisement was an inducement to singers to plug his songs, and the image of the singer on the cover helped promote the song. The first singer's image to appear on a sheet-music cover, according to Harris, was that of J. Aldrich Libbey on the cover of "After the Ball."

Harris also claimed to be the first music publisher to promote songs by planting a "stooge" in the audience. "I conceived the idea that I would have someone in the gallery start the applause. The rest of the audience would surely follow. This idea has been handed down to this very day, but I can safely state that it was the first time it was ever tried out in the history of the popular song. That was the real beginning of 'song plugging,' which means exploiting or advertising a song by calling the public's attention to it either by singing or applauding it."[10]

Still another of Harris's innovations was the illustrated song. When a singer was going to introduce one of his songs in a Milwaukee theater, Harris decided "I was going to think up a new way of exploiting this song. Instead of having him come out and sing it in the ordinary way, it was my intention to illustrate it in some manner while he was singing it." He got a scene painter to depict images from the chorus of the song on curtains that were lowered, one after the other, as the song was sung. "To my complete surprise, the audience applauded this innovation enthusiastically."[11]

Harris refined his illustrated songs after attending a travelogue lecture that was illustrated by stereopticon slides. "A new idea had occurred to me—to have actors pose for the pictures to illustrate my songs." After the actors were photographed in scenes from the lyrics, Harris had the photos transferred to glass slides that were hand-colored. The first slides also had painted backgrounds, but Harris was soon posing actors against real settings. He also added slides with the lyrics so that the audience could sing along. Soon his "song slides" were being shown in vaudeville theaters across the country, and other music publishers picked up the idea:

> This so-called fad lasted for a score of years—until the advent of the moving pictures, which soon superseded the illustrated song slides. From this it can readily be seen that the illustrated song was the forerunner of the motion picture.[12]

While this last claim may go too far, song slides were incorporated into movie houses.

Although the movies were silent, they had musical accompaniment—by pianos or violins in small-town theaters; by huge organs or even full orchestras in big-city movie palaces. Movie reels had to be changed every ten minutes, so theaters used illustrated songs—with "song slides" projected on the screen—between reel changes. According to Robert Lissauer, the first song to be "illustrated by slides and projected on a screen in a theater" was Edward B. Marks and Joseph W. Stern's "The Little Lost Child" in 1894.[13] Such incorporation of popular songs into movie theaters paved the way for the close collaboration between Tin Pan Alley and Hollywood after the advent of talking pictures in the late 1920s.

Harris was proud of the fact that, from the time he began writing songs, his lyrics had what later would come to be called "integration" between song and the story of a musical. "Here was a new idea…a song to fit the situation":

> Curiously enough, this simple idea was unheard of in those days. Songs were thrown into performances promiscuously; any kind of a song in any place or situation, so long as it afforded performers the opportunity of displaying their vocal powers. The result was that the song often had no significance. My idea, even in those early days, was never to write a song that did not fit some situation, an idea which I have adhered to ever since.[14]

In 1909, Harris was able to use his stature to help pass a copyright law that would benefit all of his fellow songwriters. As the recording industry grew, songwriters were concerned that they received no profits from the sale of recordings of their songs. Bills were introduced in Congress to protect the interests of songwriters, but they were "pigeonholed and stood no show of being passed," despite lobbying efforts by such composers as Victor Herbert and John Philip Sousa.

At this point, Harris went to Washington to ask a friend what he could do about the problem. "There is only one man to see," his musician friend advised him, "President Roosevelt, who is an author himself and will appreciate the story you have told me.... If you can get him interested, half the battle is won."

"How in the name of Heaven, am I going to meet the President?" Harris demanded. The friend said he could arrange an appointment through the post-master-general, who had formerly been Roosevelt's secretary. The next morning Harris was ushered into the office of the President by Mr. Loeb, Roosevelt's secretary, who advised Harris to "talk to him like a Dutch uncle" and take up no more than five or six minutes.

Harris continued, "He rose when we entered, and Mr. Loeb introduced me. Then he sat down, and looking me in the eye, said: 'Well?' 'I assure you, I felt like falling through the floor." But Harris presented his case for songwriters and publishers against the recording companies as powerfully—and succinctly—as he could to the president:

> Suddenly he banged his clenched fist on his desk and demanded in a loud voice: "Do you mean to tell me that you are not receiving any remuneration from the mechanical companies for the works of your brain?"
>
> "Yes, Mr. President," said I; "but you can hardly blame them, as they are within the law. We writers are working under the copyright law of 1701, which has never been changed, and the mechanical record is a device that has sprung up in the meantime and there is no clause in our copyright to cover it."
>
> "Nevertheless," said the President, "It is an injustice to use a writer's works without his being paid for them."
>
> "You are right, Mr. President; and they could use any part of the books you have written and published." [Roosevelt replied] "I should like to see them do it." He looked at me steadily for a while and then asked, "Who is drawing up this bill?"

Harris gave him a description of the stalled legislation:

> "Are you a writer?"
> "Yes, both writer and publisher, so I can talk for both sides."
> "What have you ever written?"
> "*After the Ball.*"
> "That's enough," said he. "Who is on the committee?"

Roosevelt then ordered letters to be written for Harris to be presented to the chairmen of the House and Senate committees. Harris continues, "He stood up, shook hands with me, and said: '"Mr. Harris, I am with you to the finish. Good luck!'"

He touched the button, and Secretary Loeb entered and escorted me out. I really did not know whether I was walking on my head or feet. As I was leaving, Loeb said: "You must have greatly interested the President. Do you know long you have been in there?"

"No," said I.

"Exactly forty minutes; that is longer than any one has remained in that room since I have been secretary."[15]

Even with Roosevelt's support, Harris and other songwriters had to win over recalcitrant congressmen, and a young lawyer, Nathan Burkan, had to fight against a dozen prominent attorneys hired by the record companies. In the end, however, a new copyright bill was passed in 1909 that gave Tin Pan Alley songwriters and publishers royalties from the sale of recordings of their songs.

For all of his success, Charles K. Harris remained tied to nineteenth-century song traditions. He clung to the strophic song-story formula that alternated between verses that rendered a narrative, and refrains that punctuated that narrative with a repeated lyrical exclamation. For example, Harris's "Just Behind the Times" (1896) bewailed the forced retirement of an old-fashioned minister; "Break the News to Mother" (1897) had started out as a Civil War song about a boy's dying words after enlisting at the urging of his sweetheart but over the objections of his parents. But since America had not been at war in many years, Harris shelved "Break the News to Mother" but took it down again and changed it to a song about a fireman's dying words after fighting to save a burning building. The song was not a hit, but after the outbreak of the Spanish-American War, Harris shrewdly changed the fireman back to a dying soldier, and sales took off. Harris's last hit gave voice to a little boy who longs for his dead mother as he suffers under a stepmother who constantly scolds him for being "Always in the Way" (1903). After that, however, his career declined until his death in 1930. Musically, he clung to the waltz and upheld the Victorian standard of elevated diction in his lyrics, advising aspiring songwriters to "avoid slang." Like the minister depicted in one of his lyrics, Charles K. Harris fell "Just Behind the Times."

While his success as a songwriter ebbed, Harris never lost his mastery of salesmanship. When Johnny Mercer was just starting out as a lyricist, he and his new wife Ginger lived with her mother in Brooklyn. Every day Mercer would try to peddle his songs to Tin Pan Alley publishers. "I had twenty-five cents a day," he recalled. "I'd take the subway over for a nickel, have two hot dogs and an orange drink (fifteen cents) for lunch, and use the last nickel to take the subway back to Brooklyn for supper." One day as Mercer was walking along Broadway, he noticed a sign on a second-story window that read "Charles K. Harris Music Co."

As a kid, Mercer idolized songwriters, so he knew Harris as the composer of "After the Ball." Mercer went on, "I timidly climbed the stairs to see what a music company looked like, and perhaps a real live songwriter as well. To my surprise, there was no secretary, and I was greeted by a little, old gray-haired cat in his seventies, or perhaps even older, with a cordial, 'What can I do for you, young man?' "

Mercer told Harris he was a fan of his songs, and the composer regaled him with stories of his triumphs, which included going "down the line" in Chicago (visiting all the high-priced bordellos on State Street). Mercer grew bored but, "being a polite Southern lad," sat through more stories, including the fact that Harris had recently written a book about his career.

> "Indeed?" I inquired politely.
> "Oh, yes. Would you like an autographed copy?"
> "I'd be honored," I replied.

Whereupon, with much flourish and in an elegant, Spenserian hand, Harris wrote extravagantly upon the flyleaf: 'To my good and dear friend, Johnny Mercer, with the best wishes of the Author, Charles K. Harris.'" As Harris escorted Johnny Mercer to the door, he said "quite clearly, 'That'll be two dollars!'"

At the time, Mercer recalled, "I had only about three dollars to my name."[16]

Ragtime

———————⟨◆◆◆⟩———————

THE CHICAGO WORLD'S FAIR of 1893 not only helped "After the Ball" become the biggest hit Tin Pan Alley had yet seen, it introduced Americans to a new kind of music. Ragtime was a syncopated piano style that had emerged from the red-light districts of New Orleans, St. Louis, and all points between on the Mississippi River. The ragtime pianist would maintain a steady *oom-pah* rhythm with the left hand, reminiscent of a march beat, while the right hand came in slightly before or after those regular beats, "ragging" the rhythm with syncopation. Tin Pan Alley quickly seized upon the popularity of ragtime by creating what were then termed "coon songs"—vernacular, comic songs that resembled minstrel show numbers. These songs were frequently performed by "coon shouters," hefty white women in blackface, such as Marie Cahill and May Irwin. These "queens of American musical comedy," Gerald Bordman notes, "belted out their songs to the farthest reaches of a theatre."[1]

Most coon songs were written by white songwriters, though some were written by blacks, such as Ernest Hogan. Hogan, whose real name was Reuben Crowder; adopted "Ernest Hogan" because it made him sound Irish and capitalized on the popularity of Irish songs. In 1896, he ignited the coon-song fad with "All Coons Look Alike to Me." The lyric, as David Jasen and Gene Jones point out, "are the parting words of the singer's girlfriend. She has left him for another man, so all coons (that is, *all men*) look alike to her, except her new beau. The words are no more of-fensive than those of a hundred other coon songs, but the title of Hogan's song struck a nerve. He had accidentally capsulized one of the baser tenets of prejudice that all blacks are alike and need not be thought of as individuals."[2] Although Hogan would later regret writing "All Coons Look Alike to Me," the song quickly sold more than a million copies of sheet music and spawned hundreds of other coon songs.

Unlike minstrel songs that look back nostalgically on rural plantation life, coon songs portrayed blacks as pugnacious, mercenary, and sexually aggressive.

As Jasen and Jones observe, "They have an urban, in-your-face toughness that borders on belligerence. The minstrel songs strut; coon songs swagger."[3] Coon songs brought in a new syncopated musical idiom and a lyrical style Charles K. Harris warned songwriters to avoid—slang. Setting colloquial lyrics to even mildly syncopated music steered coon songs away from the strophic pattern of nineteenth-century song. Instead of telling a story through a series of verses, coon songs merely sketched a situation in one or two verses and concentrated on a lyrical refrain in which a caricatured black might plead "I Want Yer, Ma Honey" (1895), celebrate "My Black Baby Mine" (1896), or lament the loss of his woman's sexual appetite in "You Been a Good Old Wagon But You Done Broke Down" (1896). Not only did such coon songs create a shift from sentimental narrative ballads, such as "After the Ball," to more "lyrical" effusions, the use of dialect made the words themselves more playfully prominent. In Ben Harney's "Mister Johnson, Turn Me Loose" (1896), for example, listeners were delighted by the idiomatic plea of the singer to "Mister Johnson" (slang for the police):

> Oh, Mister Johnson, turn me loose!
> Don't take me to the calaboose!

The lyrics of the coon song, as Isaac Goldberg observed, "were as different from the words of the waltz-tragedies as was the music of those waltzes from the jagged melodies of the raging 'rags.'" When those lyrics turned to love, they created what Goldberg termed a "vocabulary of unadorned passion—a crude *ars amandi*."[4] Thus with a forthrightness unimaginable in a sentimental ballad, a coon song "shouter" could plead, "All I want is lovin'—I don't want your money."

But soon the ragtime coon song began mingling its vernacular idioms with the elevated diction of the sentimental waltz ballad. Such stylistic clashes as "yon nig" color Ernest Hogan's lyrics, and, in Barney Fagan's "My Gal Is a High Born Lady" (1896), a black bridegroom looks forward to his wedding day in these slangy as well as elegant terms:

> Sunny Africa's Four Hundred's gwine to be thar,
> To do honor to my lovely fiancée;
> Thar' will be a grand ovation
> Of especial ostentation

Kerry Mills's "At a Georgia Camp Meeting" (1897) shows the same stylistic schizophrenia, suddenly switching from "how the Sisters did shout" to "'Twas so entrancing." By the turn of the century, one might say of the coon song the same thing one of its caricatured lovers says of his "baby"—"She's Getting Mo' Like the White Folks Every Day" (1901):

> Now she can sing "The Swanee River"
> Like it was never sung before,

But since she's worked in that hotel
She warbles "Il Trovatore."

Some of these songs barely sound like coon songs today; only if one listens carefully to the words (or sees the sheet music cover adorned with racist caricatures) does their heritage betray itself. Still, their vernacular punch, their comic touches, and their passionate flair were a refreshing change from the sentimental ballads of the 1890s. For the most part, moreover, these ragtime songs were not strophic narratives in which a story unfolded in a series of verses punctuated by a short lyrical refrain of eight or sixteen bars. The verse increasingly served merely as an introduction to the refrain, which was lengthening to a "chorus" of thirty-two bars.

Even today, one can still hear such ragtime coon songs as "Hello, Ma Baby" (1899). The only touches that would have marked "Hello, Ma Baby" as a coon song to its original listeners were slang and dialect phrases such as "ma baby" (in coon songs, "baby" referred to a black woman) and "tell me I'se your own," as well as the exuberant expression of romantic passion that would not have been deemed appropriate for white lovers:

Send me a kiss by wire,
Baby, my heart's on fire!

Joseph E. Howard and Ida Emerson refresh the standard telephone greeting by "ragging"—reversing—the verbal accent against the musical beat: not the normally accented "Hel-**lo**" but "**Hel**-lo." They also use feminine rhymes (two-syllable rhymes in which the accent falls on the next to the last syllable, leaving the final syllable "effeminately" weak and unaccented):

*If you re-**fuse** me,*
*Honey, you'll **lose** me*

Poets from Byron through W. S. Gilbert have found feminine rhymes create comic effects more effectively than masculine rhymes, in which the final syllable is accented ("a-**lone**" / "**own**").

The musical and lyrical structure of "Hello, Ma Baby" is a distinct departure from nineteenth-century strophic songs. Both verse and chorus are sixteen measures long, striking a balance between the two parts of the song as opposed to the preponderance of verses in earlier songs. And the verses don't tell a story so much as set up the chorus as the main part of the song: one verse ends with "And this is what I say to baby mine"; the other with "And so each day I shout along the line." Both verses serve as introductions to the chorus rather than strophic segments of a developing narrative. Thus "Hello, Ma Baby," like so many later songs, can be performed by dropping the verses altogether and singing only the chorus.

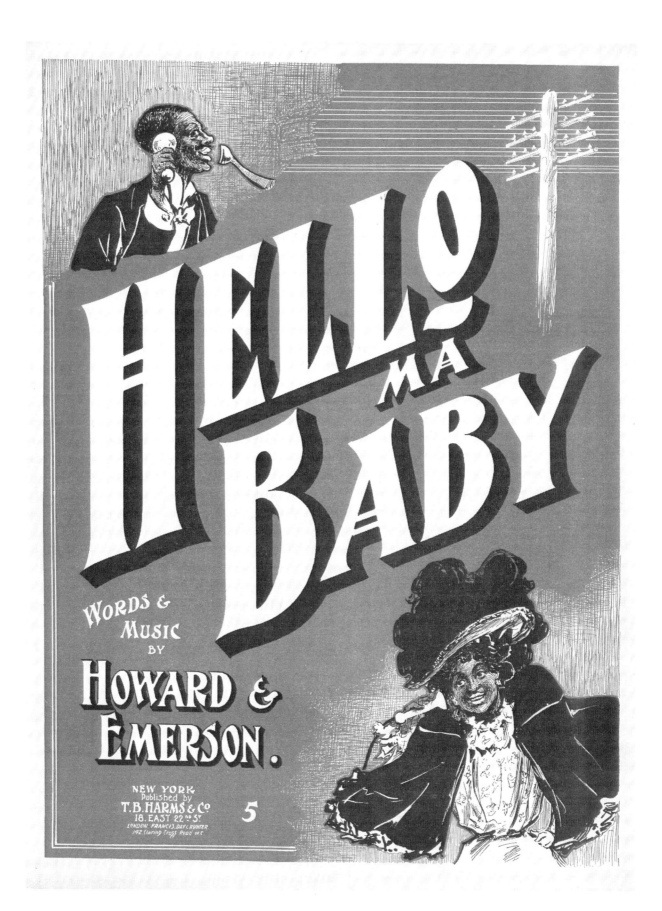

HELLO! MA BABY.

By Howard and Emerson.

4

nev - er seen my hon - ey but she's mine, all right; So
sat - is - fied be - cause I'se got my babe's ad - dress, Here

take my tip, an leave this gal a - lone.
past - ed in the lin - ing of my hat.

Ev' - ry sin - gle morn - ing, you will hear me yell, "Hey
I am might - y scared, 'cause if the wires get crossed, 'Twill

Cen - tral! fix me up a - long the line." He con -
sep - a - rate me from ma ba - by mine, Then some

Hello! ma Baby. 4

-nects me with ma hon - ey, then I rings the bell, And
oth - er coon will win her, and my game is lost, And

this is what I say to ba - by mine, ...
so each day I shout a - long the line, ...

CHORUS

"Hel - lo! ma ba - by, Hel - lo! ma hon - ey,

Hel - lo! ma rag - time gal, ... Send me a kiss by

Hello! ma Baby. 4

Hello! ma Baby. 4

30

While some ragtime coon songs such as "Hello, Ma Baby" could shed their racist caricatures over time, others have indelibly retained them. "Bill Bailey, Won't You Please Come Home?" for example, still bristles with stereotypes of the philandering black man and the woman who nevertheless loves him. Those stereotypes are reflected in the racist caricatures depicted on the cover of the sheet music (though the singers, whose photograph appears on the cover, are white).

In "Bill Bailey," syncopated musical phrases "rag" the lyric into verbal shards:

'Member dat
Rainy eve dat
I drove you out
Wid nothing but
A fine tooth comb?

Such an anguished, erotic plea for a lover's return would have been unthinkable in a sentimental ballad for whites, but soon such passion—and humor—worked their ways into mainstream lyrics.

Bill Bailey, Won't You Please Come Home?

Words and Music by HUGHIE CANNON.

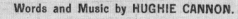

On one sum-mer's day........
Bill drove by dat door.......

Sun was shin-ing fine,........ The la - dy love of old Bill Bail-ey was hanging clothes on de
In an au-to-mo - bile,........ A great big dia - mond, coach- and foot - man, hear dat big wench

line In 'her back yard,.................. and weep - ing hard;.................. She
squeal; "He's all a - lone,".............. I heard her groan;.................. She

married a B. and O. brakeman, Dat took and throw'd her down, Beller-ing like a prune-fed calf, wid a
hol - lered thro' that door, "Bill Bai-ley, is you sore? Stop a minute; won't you listen to me? Won't

big gang hang-ing 'round; And to dat crowd,............ She yelled out loud:...............
I see you no more?" Bill winked his eye,.............. As he heard her cry:..................

Bill Bailey, Won't You Please Come Home? 4 pp — 2d p.

"YOU WERE NEVER INTRODUCED TO ME"
By NAT. BIVIN.

A splendid coon song by the author of "I Ain't Seen No Messenger Boy." The above song is
now being featured by all star singers and is sure to be a winner.

CHORUS.

Won't you come home, Bill Bai - ley, won't you come home? She moans de

whole day long;............... I'll do de cook - ing, dar - ling,

I'll pay de rent; I knows I've done you wrong;.............

Bill Bailey, Won't You Please Come Home? 4 pp — 3d p.

"APPEARANCES, DEY SEEM TO BE AGAINST ME."

By GARDENIER & KOHLMAN.

Something new in a darky song and a positive hit.   Words very catchy, music entrancing.
Secure a copy, you will not regret it.

'Mem-ber dat rain-y eve dat I drove you out, Wid noth-ing but a fine tooth

comb?........... I knows I'se to blame; well, ain't dat a shame? Bill

1. **2.**

Bai-ley, won't you please come home?........ home?...........

Bill Bailey, Won't You Please Come Home? 4 pp — 4th p.

Geo. Beaverson, 35 Frankfort St., N. Y.

PING PONG LANCIERS
Arranged by THEO. F. MORSE.

is one of the best medley lanciers on the market to-day and contains such hits as
"**Ain't That A Shame**," "Little Boy in Blue," "Come Out, Dinah, on the Green," "My Princess Zulu Lulu"
"Bill Bailey, Won't You Please Come Home?" "Way Down in Old Indiana."

36

Bob Cole and
J. Rosamond and James
Weldon Johnson

IT WAS, IN FACT, a team of black songwriters who nurtured the hybrid of coon song and sentimental ballad. By making its lyrics "noticeably more genteel," J. Rosamond Johnson, his brother James Weldon Johnson, and Bob Cole were hailed as a collective "Moses" who led "the coon song into the promised land." In "Under the Bamboo Tree," the writers, according to Rosamond Johnson himself, tried to "clean up the caricature," using only "mild dialect" to express love "in phrases universal enough" to meet the "genteel demands of middle-class America."[1] It was lyricist Bob Cole who suggested to Johnson that the spiritual "Nobody Knows the Trouble I've Seen" could be turned into a ragtime song. Johnson at first thought the suggestion sacrilegious, but, at Cole's insistence, he syncopated the spiritual. In the lyric, Cole placed his lovers in Africa, where he could sidestep the coon caricature by having a dignified "Zulu from Matabooloo" propose to a demure "maid of royal blood though dusky shade." Cole concocted what Sigmund Spaeth called "a brand new synthetic dialect":[2]

> *If you lak-a-me,*
> *Lak I lak-a-you,*
> *And we lak-a-both the same,*
> *I lak-a-say,*
> *This very day,*
> *I lak-a change your name*

Here, too, one can see another feature of ragtime songs unheard of in the sentimental ballad—deliberately using the music to distort or "rag" the lyric. Turning the one-syllable "like" into the two-syllable "lak-a" gave Cole a verbal equivalent for the syncopated eighth-note/sixteenth-note pattern in the music. It also inspired him to create something few sentimental "song-story" balladeers would ever bother with—a pun, and a triple pun at that: on "like" meaning *wish* ("I lak-a change your name"), *love* ("If you lak-a me"), and—in what would become Tin Pan Alley's favorite grammatical error—"like" in place of "as" ("lak I lak-a you"). Using music to "rag'" words—reversing verbal patterns, breaking up phrases, splitting syllables—would later become prominent features in the lyrics of Ira Gershwin, Lorenz Hart, Yip Harburg, and other lyricists.

"Under the Bamboo Tree" was the biggest hit for Cole and the Johnson brothers. It was interpolated into *Sally in Our Alley* where it was sung by Marie Cahill and quickly became her signature song. As David Jasen and Gene Jones note, it "inspired a new genre of pop writing: the "jungle song" ("Down in Jungle Town," "By the Light of the Jungle Moon," "Aba Daba Honeymoon," and many others)."[3] "Under the Bamboo Tree" was revived for the 1944 MGM musical *Meet Me in St. Louis*, where, with a new arrangement by Hugh Martin, it was given a rousing performance by Judy Garland and Margaret O'Brien.

Whether "Under the Bamboo Tree" cleaned up—or merely transplanted—the racist caricatures of the ragtime coon song, it certainly made for an artful blend of lyric and music that achieved its effects not by sentimental storytelling but by a clever fit (and sometimes even more cleverly ragged misfit) between verbal and musical phrasing. Its colloquial ease, moreover, offered a new idiom for romantic expression—a cut above the dialect of the coon song yet still well below the high-flown style of such ponderous narratives as "A Bird in a Gilded Cage" (1900). The ragtime coon song, as Max Morath has argued, began "transcending its racial slur and dialect" and "licensing the use of slang and colloquialism, even bad grammar."[4]

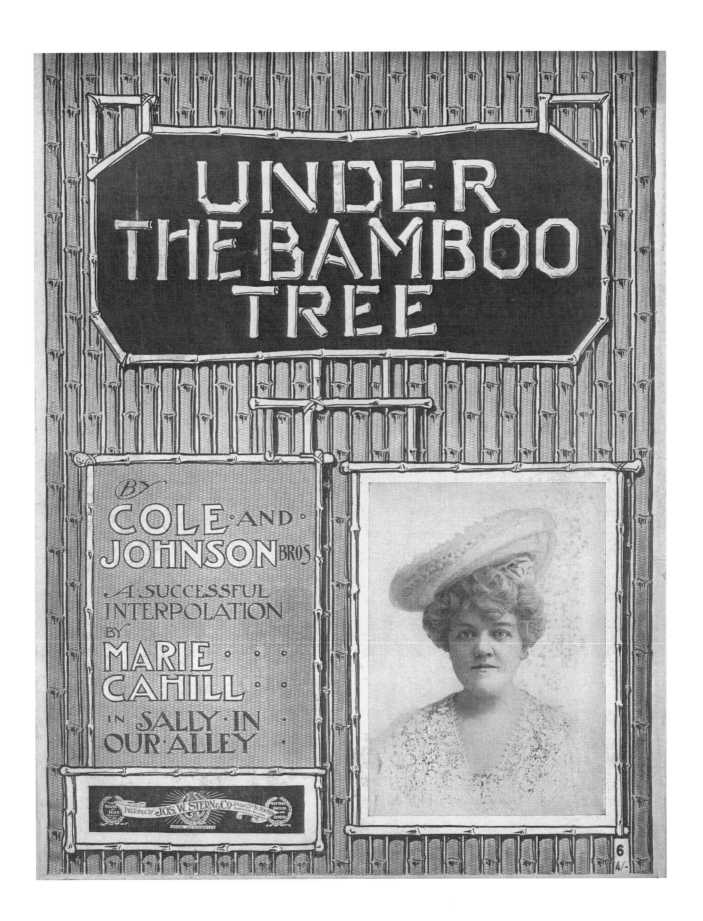

UNDER THE BAMBOO TREE.

by BOB COLE.

1. Down in the jun-gles lived a maid   Of roy-al blood though
2. And in this sim-ple jun-gle way,   He wooed the maid-en
3. This lit-tle sto-ry strange but true,   Is of-ten told in

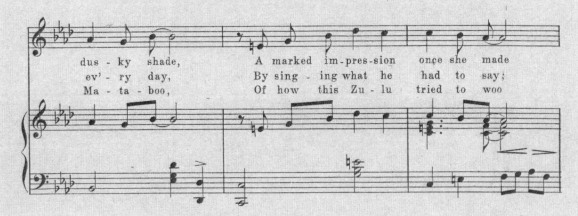

dus-ky shade,   A marked im-pres-sion once she made
ev'-ry day,   By sing-ing what he had to say;
Ma-ta-boo,   Of how this Zu-lu tried to woo

Copyright MCMII by Jos. W. Stern & Co.

8384-3

4

Chorus.   *not fast*.

not fast.

p-f

If you lak - a-me, lak I lak - a-you, And we lak - a-both the

same,   I lak - a say,   this ve-ry day,   I lak-a-change your name;   'Cause

I love-a-you and love-a-you true And if you-a love-a-me,

One live as two,   two live as one   Un-der the bam-boo tree.   If   tree.

sfz

D.S.

George M. Cohan

A KEY FIGURE IN the spread of ragtime syncopation and vernacular lyrics was George M. Cohan. Although he may not, as his lyric for "The Yankee Doodle Boy" claimed, have been born exactly "on the Fourth of July," it was close enough. More telling was that his parents were performing at a theater in Providence, and George Michael Cohan was born in the wings on July 3, 1878. He traveled the vaudeville circuit with his family and made his first stage appearance at eight years old. Soon he was performing in an act of his own, "Master Georgie—Violin Tricks and Tinkling Tunes," earning the nickname "that Cohan brat" from other performers. Taking over the family act of "The Four Cohans," Georgie decided that they needed to get out of vaudeville and move up to the "legitimate" theater.

While his early songs, such as "When the Girl You Love Is Many Miles Away (1893) are mired in the sentimental ballad tradition, Cohan quickly embraced ragtime. Knowing that the code words for sex in coon songs were "hot" and "warm"—"Dar's No Coon Warm Enough for Me," "A Hot Coon from Memphis," "A Red Hot Coon"—Cohan contributed his own "The Warmest Baby in the Bunch" (1896). He then reversed the formula with "You're Growing Cold, Cold, Cold" (1898), advertised as "the story of a coon with an iceberg heart."

Although he soon dropped such racist motifs, Cohan was determined to bring ragtime's jaunty rhythms and vernacular lyrics to Broadway. At the time, Broadway was dominated by European models—Viennese operetta, French *opéra bouffe*, and the comic operettas of Gilbert and Sullivan. Cohan used ragtime songs to give Broadway an infusion of American fresh air. Although *Little Johnny Jones* (1904) at first fared poorly on stage, Cohan peddled its songs directly on Tin Pan Alley and turned several of them into hits.

In "Give My Regards to Broadway," Cohan employs the ragtime device of matching short and long vowels to the eighth-note/quarter-note pattern. He also uses musical phrasing to truncate verbal phrasing and create lyrical shards with surprising rhymes:

> *Give my regards to Broadway,*
> *Remember me to Herald Square*
> *Tell all the gang at*
> *Forty-second Street that*
> *I will soon be there.*

To give voice to such homegrown sentiments, Cohan created a persona—an insouciant, urbane New Yorker, as brash as the city he celebrates. Because he wrote the book as well as music and lyrics for his shows, he could integrate songs more closely into story and character than they were in most Broadway musicals of his day. When critics assailed "his excessive dependence on slang, Cohan retorted that that was the way his characters would talk could they have come to life off stage. He was not writing 'literature,' he was creating an entertainment about people with whom his audience could identify."[1]

"Give My Regards To Broadway."

GEO. M. COHAN.

Did you ev - er
Say hel - lo to

see two Yan-kees part up - on a for - eign
dear old Con - ey Isle, if there you chance to

shore, _____ When the good ship's just a - bout to
be, _____ When you're at the Wal - dorf have a

start for Old New York once more? _____ With
smile and charge it up to me; _____ Men-tion

tear - dimmed eye they say good - bye, they're friends with
my name ev - 'ry place you go, as 'round the

out a doubt; _____ When the man on the pier
town you roam; _____ Wish you'd call on my gal, Now re -

Shouts,"Let them clear," as the ship strikes out. _____
mem - ber, old pal, when you get back home. _____

Give my regards to Broadway. 4

CHORUS.

Give my re-gards to Broad - - way, re-mem - ber me to Her - ald Square,

Tell all the gang at For - ty - Sec-ond street, that I will soon be there;

Give my regards to Broadway. 4

Give my regards to Broadway. 4

Cohan could also transform America's oldest popular song into an urbane and energetic "I Am" song. In the original "Yankee Doodle," a country bumpkin sticks a feather in his cap and calls it "macaroni"—a slang term for elegant attire. During the Revolutionary War, British soldiers sang the song derisively to caricature colonists who thought that by simply sticking a feather in their caps, they could attain the height of fashion. When Cornwallis surrendered to George Washington at Yorktown, however, the band exuberantly played "Yankee Doodle Dandy." In the same cocksure spirit, Cohan's "Yankee Doodle Boy" flaunts his "dandified" sophistication:

> *I'm a Yankee Doodle dandy,*
> *A Yankee Doodle do or die.*
> *A real, live nephew of my Uncle Sam,*
> *Born on the Fourth of July.*

The song has become known as "Yankee Doodle Dandy," after the 1942 film in which James Cagney portrayed Cohan brilliantly and helped his songs become part of *The American Song Book.*

The YANKEE DOODLE BOY

ONE OF THE MUSICAL HITS from GEO. M. COHAN'S LATEST PLAY

"LITTLE JOHNNY JONES"

Words & Music by GEO. M. COHAN

THE YANKEE DOODLE COMEDIAN

F. A. MILLS
48 WEST 29TH ST.
NEW YORK

"The Yankee Doodle Boy."

GEO. M. COHAN.

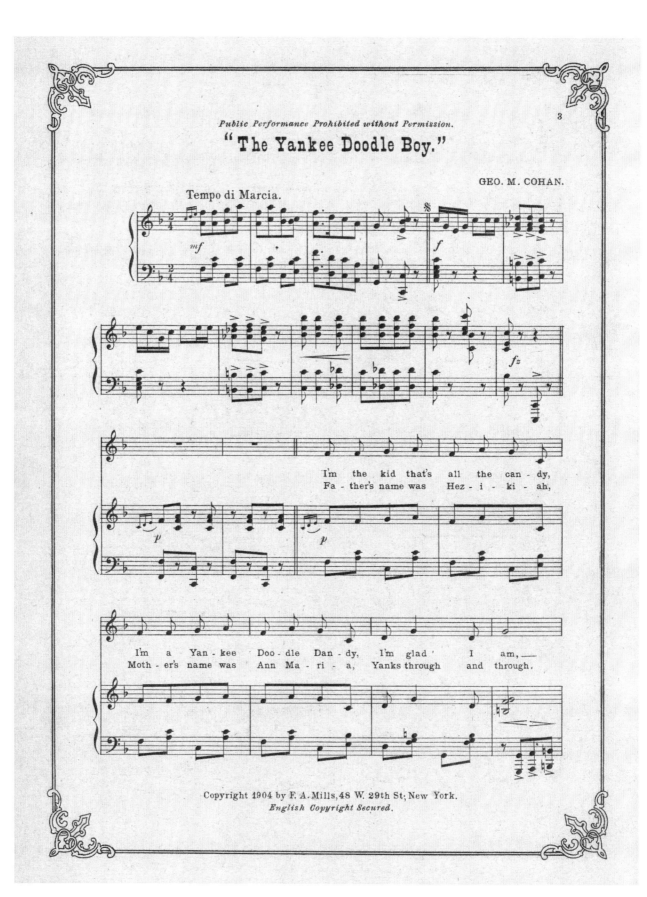

Tempo di Marcia.

I'm the kid that's all the can - dy,
Fa - ther's name was Hez - i - ki - ah,

I'm a Yan - kee Doo - dle Dan - dy, I'm glad I am, ___
Moth - er's name was Ann Ma - ri - a, Yanks through and through.

that ain't a josh, She's a Yan - kee, by gosh. *CHO.* (Oh,
that's go - ing some, For the Yan - kees, by gum. *CHO.* (Oh,

say can you see _____ An - y -
say can you see _____ An - y -

thing a - bout a Yan - kee that's a phon - - ey?)
thing a - bout my ped - i - gree that's phon - - ey?)

Yankee Doodle Boy. 5

5

6

CHORUS.

I'm a Yan - kee Doo - dle Dan - - dy, A

Yan - kee Doo - dle, do or die; _____ A

real live nep - hew of my Un - cle Sam's,

Born on the Fourth of Ju - ly. _____ I've

Yankee Doodle Boy. 5

7

Yankee Doodle Boy, 5

In Cohan's hands, ragtime songs metamorphosed into the casual ease of a jaunty cosmopolite who could even salute the flag in slang. Cohan had heard a Civil War veteran solemnly refer to the flag with the phrase "she's a grand old rag." But when he used the phrase as a song title, people thought referring to Old Glory as a "rag" was disrespectful. Complaints from patriotic societies and even an order from President Cleveland forced him to revise his original lyric from "You're a Grand Old Rag" to "You're a Grand Old Flag." Still, Cohan's brusque New Yorker sidestepped solemn patriotism with jagged musical and verbal phrases:

You're the emblem of
The land I love
The home of
The free and the brave.

Such abrupt fragments disclose surprising rhymes on *land* and *and*, *em-* and *-blem*, and *of* and *love*—a desperate maneuver in a language that has fewer rhymes for "love" than almost any other four-letter word. French has fifty-one rhymes for *amour*, including some wonderful ones such as *toujours*, but the Germanic English language has only five—"dove," "above," "glove, "shove," and, in a pinch, "of."

YOU'RE A GRAND OLD FLAG

A SONG-HIT
FROM
THE LATEST
MUSICAL PLAY

GEORGE WASHINGTON JR.

WRITTEN AND
COMPOSED BY

GEO. M. COHAN

5

F.A.MILLS
48 WEST 29TH ST
NEW YORK

"You're A Grand Old Flag."

GEO. M. COHAN.

tune like "Yan - kee Doo - dle" simp - ly sets me off my noo - dle, It's that
don't be - lieve in rav - ing ev - 'ry time I see it wav - ing. There's a

pa - tri - ot - ic some - thing that no one can un - der - stand.
chill runs up my back that makes me glad I'm what I am.

Chorus.   Solo.
"Way down South in the land of cot - ton," mel - o - dy un -
Here's a land with a mil - lion sol - diers, that's_____ if we should

tir - ing,_____ Ain't that in - spir - ing!_____ Hur - rah! Hur -
need 'em,_____ We'll fight for free - dom!_____ Hur - rah! Hur -

Chorus.

You're a grand old flag. 4

You're a grand old flag.4

61

peace may you wave._____ You're the em- blem of the land I love, The

home of the free and the brave,_____ Ev -'ry heart beats true under Red, White and

Blue, Where there's nev - er a boast or brag; _____ "But should auld ac-quain-tance

be for-got," Keep your eye on the grand old flag. You're a flag._____

For years, Cohan was one of the few vernacular voices on Broadway. Franz Lehár, Rudolf Friml, and Victor Herbert "led the American public," as Leonard Bernstein put it, "straight into the arms of operetta," with its exotic settings, melodramatic plots, lush music, and "stilted and overelegant lyrics."[2] Only a few songs from operettas, such as "Ah! Sweet Mystery of Life" (1910), became independently popular through sheet-music sales. But by 1910, songs from Tin Pan Alley began to go beyond ephemeral popularity to become the enduring "standards" that form *The American Song Book*.

Shelton Brooks

——————◆—◆—◆——————

SHELTON BROOKS was a black songwriter who was born in Ontario, moved to Cleveland as a child, and settled in Chicago in his twenties. He placed his songs with Will Rossiter, the self-styled "Chicago publisher." "By automatically giving Rossiter the first look at his work," note David Jasen and Gene Jones, "Brooks escaped the grind of peddling his songs."[1] As a songwriter who wrote both music and lyrics, Brooks came up with a melody in 1910 but couldn't think of a lyric to go with it. "One afternoon he heard a couple quarreling. 'Better not walk out on me, man!' said the angry woman, 'for some of these days you're gonna miss me, honey.' The song words then fell into place."[2]

But because Brooks's most recent song had not done well, Rossiter declined to publish "Some of These Days." Brooks then took it to William Foster, an African-American publisher who would go on to become one of the first black film producers. Foster asked Brooks to contribute thirty-five dollars to the roughly thirteen hundred dollars it took to print and promote a song. Brooks agreed and also plugged the song himself.

While the sheet music indicates it was introduced by Blossom Seeley, Brooks tried to demonstrate the song for Sophie Tucker, at that time a blackface "coon shouter" who was playing at a vaudeville theater in Chicago. When Tucker refused to see him, Brooks turned to Mollie Elkins, her black maid. Elkins beseeched Tucker to give Brooks a hearing. When Tucker heard Shelton Brooks sing "Some of These Days," she said she could have kicked herself for nearly missing out on the song:

> It had everything... I've turned it inside out, singing it every way imaginable, as a dramatic song, as a novelty number, as a sentimental ballad, and always audiences have loved it and asked for it. "Some of These Days" is one of the great

songs that will be remembered and sung for years and years to come, like some of Stephen Foster's.[3]

If Sophie Tucker helped "Some of These Days," the song's success helped her. She had been told that she was not attractive enough to appear as herself so must don blackface. But once when her trunk was lost, she had to go on stage without her black-face makeup. When she sang "Some of These Days," the audience adored her, and she could discard her blackface mask.

"Some of These Days" doesn't sound like a song from 1910—particularly when you compare it to other songs from that year, such as "Let Me Call You Sweetheart" and "Down by the Old Mill Stream." Composer Alec Wilder called it a "landmark in popular music, perhaps *the* landmark…of its time."[4] "Some of These Days" is a clear departure from the strophic story-songs of the nineteenth century. It depicts angry, passionate lovers in lyrics such as "You'll miss my hugging / You'll miss my kissing," that would never have been uttered by the demure lovers in sentimental ballads. "Some of These Days" has the musical form of most popular songs that would follow it. There is a verse that sketches a story about how a boy has "listened to the gossips" about the promiscuity of his girlfriend and broken off their affair and left town. In the second verse, he misses her so much that he returns but is still haunted by what she said when he first deserted her. The two verses hint at a story but mostly function as an introduction to the much more lyrical and passionate chorus.

That chorus opens, stunningly, in a minor key. Like most popular songs that followed it, the chorus is thirty-two bars long, divided into four eight-bar sections. But where most later songs would use two melodies, an "A" melody and a "B" melody in an ABAB or, more commonly, an AABA pattern, "Some of These Days" uses four distinct melodies in an ABCD pattern so that no melodic eight-bar section is repeated. The musical power of the chorus comes from the three sustained pick-up notes: "Some—of—these—" that precede the climactic "days" held for five beats as it shifts from the A-sharp on "of" to an A-natural.

The title phrase is a variant of the vernacular catchphrase "one of these days" and suggests that the boy will regret his desertion not "one day" but for many days. The chorus is laced with sensuous imagery:

> *You'll miss my hugging,*
> *You'll miss my kissing,*

It also suggests that the two lovers have had a sexual relationship:

> *For you know, honey,*
> *You've had your way,*

Having "had his way" with the singer gave credence to what the "gossips" said about her. But his role in the verse of the song pales against her passionate, angry voice in the chorus. Sophie Tucker deepened that passion by changing "You'll miss your little baby" to "You'll miss your red-hot mama."

Once he learned that Sophie Tucker would use the song in her act, Will Rossiter bought "Some of These Days" from William Foster. It was the number one song for nine consecutive weeks in the fall of 1910 and was the second most popular song of that year, topped only by "Meet Me Tonight in Dreamland."[5] Over the next few years, it would sell more than two million copies of sheet music.

Some Of These Days.

By SHELTON BROOKS
Author of "You aint talking to me" etc

Copyright, MCMX, by Will Rossiter, Chicago, Ill.

best of all, So hon ey don't you go a - way, _____ Just as he went to go,
girl was gone So down he rush-es to the train _____ While it was pull-ing out,

rall

it grieved the girl - ie so These words he heard her say. _____
he heard his girl - ie shout This lov - ing sweet re - frain _____

rall

CHORUS

p-f

Some of these days _____ You'll miss me hon - ey _____ Some of these

pf

days _____ You'll feel so lone - ly _____ You'll miss my

Some of these days 4-2

Some of these days 4-3

70

Irving Berlin

IRVING BERLIN, BORN Israel Isidor Beilin/Baline in 1888, fled Russia with his family after Cossacks burned their village in a pogrom. He arrived in America in 1893, when he was just five years old. The Balines lived in the hideous poverty of New York's Lower East Side; their first apartment didn't even have a window. Moses Baline, who had been a cantor in Russia, worked as a kosher meat inspector, then as a housepainter, and the grueling job led to his death when his youngest son was only thirteen. "Izzy," along with his older brothers and sisters, worked at odd jobs to help the family make ends meet. He sold newspapers along the East River; one day a ship loading cargo swung its crane across the dock and knocked him into the river. As sailors fished him out, Izzy still clutched three pennies in his fist. When he got home that night, he proudly dropped them into his mother's lap alongside the money his older brothers and sisters had earned.

As a teenager, Izzy decided that the best way he could help his family was to quit school, run away from home, and get a job. One thing he could do was sing, and he found that if he sang popular songs on street corners, people tossed pennies to him. After spending several nights sleeping on sidewalks and park benches, he finally landed the job of his dreams—a singing waiter in a Chinatown saloon. His specialty was improvising dirty lyrics to current popular songs, and that got a lot of coins tossed his way.

One day the saloon owner, miffed that a rival establishment had written a hit song called "My Mariucci Take a Steamboat," ordered Izzy and the piano player to write a song of their own. They came up with another Italian number, "Marie from Sunny Italy." Although the song earned him only thirty-seven cents in royalties, it established Izzy Baline as a published lyricist, and on its sheet-music cover was the name "I. Berlin." Whether the last name was a misprint by the publisher or chosen by himself, Izzy quickly adopted it and later expanded the "I" into "Irving."

Soon he was writing lyrics for Tin Pan Alley music publishers. One day he presented a lyric to a publisher who liked it but assumed Berlin had music to the words as well. With consummate *chutzpah*, Berlin assured the publisher he did. The publisher asked him to step into another office where a piano player was working and whistle the melody for him. In the time it took to walk across the hall, Berlin came up with a melody to fit his lyric. From then on, Irving Berlin the lyricist was also Irving Berlin the composer.

Although his musical skills were limited—he could not read or write music and learned to play the piano in only one key—F-sharp—he was one of the few songwriters of his era who wrote both lyrics and music. Another was his friend Cole Porter. They had a private joke: When a songwriting team such as Rodgers and Hart or George and Ira Gershwin had a hit, Berlin and Porter would say to each other, "Imagine! It took *two* people to write *one* song."

Berlin was so successful that in 1910 he also joined a music publishing firm and in a few years would head his own firm, Irving Berlin, Inc., making him one of the few songwriters who owned the copyrights to his songs.

In 1911, Berlin had his first monumental hit, although his accounts of how the song came into being varied. According to one account, as he was shaving one morning, a tune popped into his head. "The melody came to me right out of the air," he recalled, "in a burst of simon-pure inspiration."[1] After playing it over a few times on the piano, however, Berlin was not impressed, so he just jotted a few notes on a sheet of paper, wrote "Alexander" (a coon-song name for a black man assuming a grandiose "white" name) across the top, and filed it away.

A few days later, as he was waiting to catch a train to Florida, he was going through his files and came across the memo about "Alexander." To kill time, he completed the melody. "I wrote the whole thing in eighteen minutes," he said. "'Alexander' was done originally as an instrumental number—no words....Six months later, I wrote words to it."[2]

The lyric he set to the melody celebrated "Alexander" as a musical camp-meeting revivalist and offered to take the listener "by the hand, up to the man, up to the man, who is the leader of the band." That friendly invitation dispelled the widespread image of ragtime as devilish music that was leading young people astray and undermining the fabric of American society. In fact, Berlin's lyric even suggested that ragtime was part of the country's musical tradition when he offered "the 'Swanee River' played—in ragtime" in tribute to Stephen Foster.

That phrase is the only syncopated moment in the song and thus, some would say, its only touch of authentic ragtime. But Berlin was able to create syncopated effects by "ragging" musical rhythms against verbal ones. He used musical accents to distort the pronunciation of "natural" so that it rhymed with "call":

They can play a bugle call
Like you never heard before

*So natur*al

That you want to go to war.

Faced with the antiwar sentiment of the 1960s, Berlin updated the lyric to "so natural that you want to *hear some more*," still keeping his deft rhyme between "*natu-*" and "*that you.*"

Although it was slow to catch on, "Alexander's Ragtime Band" became the biggest hit Tin Pan Alley had yet seen. It got its first big push in Chicago vaudeville by Emma Carus (who always opened her act with, "I'm not pretty, but I'm good to my folks"). Ever since Americans were introduced to ragtime at the Chicago World's Fair of 1893, the city had remained a center for ragtime, and Berlin's song was taken up by theaters, saloons, restaurants, and dance halls, then it spread outward along the vaudeville circuit, where it was picked up by Al Jolson.

It sold a million copies of sheet music in 1911, then another million in 1912, and continued to sell for years afterward. It was the number one song from October 1911 through January 1912. The song was heard everywhere. Vaudeville acts—sometimes all the acts on the same bill—wanted to use it, newspaper cartoons poked fun at its ubiquity, and it became a truly international hit as Berlin found when he visited London and heard his cab driver whistling the melody with no idea that his passenger was the song's creator. "Alexander's Ragtime Band" has been recorded by many singers, from Bessie Smith (who "corrected" some of the dialect grammar) to Michael Feinstein (who gives it a slow, almost mournful rendition).

For Irving Berlin, the success of "Alexander's Ragtime Band" was proof of inspiration. "Do I believe in inspiration?" he said. "In having things hit you from nowhere? Big things you've never dreamed of? Occasionally—yes. I have never given Irving Berlin any credit for 'Alexander.'"[3] But "Alexander's Ragtime Band" also set a standard he would strive to maintain for the rest of his career. "My struggles didn't actually begin until after I'd written 'Alexander's Ragtime Band,'" he said. "It's been a struggle ever since to keep success going."[4]

ALEXANDER'S RAGTIME BAND

Words and Music
By IRVING BERLIN

Oh, ma hon-ey,   Oh, ma hon-ey,
Oh, ma hon-ey,   Oh, ma hon-ey,

Bet-ter hur-ry and let's me-an-der,   Ain't you go-in',   Ain't you go-in'
There's a fid-dle with notes that screeches,   Like a chick-en,   Like a chick-en,

To   the lead-er man,   rag-ged me-ter man?   Oh, ma hon-ey,
And   the clar-in-et   is   a col-ored pet,   Come and lis-ten,

Copyright 1911 by Ted Snyder Co. Inc. 112 W 38th St. N.Y.

International Copyright Secured

3
Oh, ma hon-ey, Let me take you to Al-ex-an-der's
Come and lis-ten, To a class-i-cal band what's peach-es,
grand stand, brass band, Ain't you com-in' a-long?
come now, some-how, Bet-ter hur-ry a-long.
CHORUS
Come on and hear, Come on and hear Al-ex-an-der's rag-time
p-f
band, Come on and hear, Come on and hear, It's the best band in the
Alexander's Ragtime Band 4

land,.......... They can play a bu–gle call like you nev–er heard be–fore,

So nat–ur–al that you want to go to war; That's just the

best–est band what am, hon–ey lamb, Come on a–

long,............ Come on a - long,................ Let me take you by the

Alexander's Ragtime Band 4

The Dance Craze

THE SUCCESS OF "Alexander's Ragtime Band" helped fuel the dance craze that swept across America in the wake of ragtime. Just as, a century before, the waltz had shocked society by inviting dancers to touch and hold one another in a manner never permitted in the more courtly minuets and gavottes of the eighteenth century, so twentieth-century's ragtime spawned new dances in which couples grasped, embraced, and even hugged each other. With such animalistic names as the Turkey Trot, the Bunny Hug, the Grizzly Bear, the Chicken Scratch, the Buzzard Lope, and the Monkey Glide, these new dances emanated from black dives and red-light districts. They relied upon ragtime syncopation for their frenzied and suggestive steps, steps based on a walk or shuffle, placing more emphasis on bodily movement than traditional dances, which concentrated on patterns for the feet.

Even as late as 1910, it was considered unseemly for refined adults to be seen dancing in public rather than at parties in private homes. But between 1912 and 1914, more than one hundred new dances were introduced that had young and old dancing on almost a daily basis. Lamenting "The Revolt of Decency," the *New York Sun* echoed the common assumption that all of the dances were originated by blacks and were not "new" at all but "based on the primitive motive of orgies enjoyed by the aboriginal inhabitants of every uncivilized land."[1]

The dance craze flourished in newly fashionable cabarets. As F. Scott Fitzgerald, chronicler of the Jazz Age, later observed, the dance craze "brought the nice girl into the café, thus beginning a profound revolution in American life."[2] Restaurant owners, eager to bolster business in the economically depressed days of 1911, took steps to mingle dining and dancing. Julius Keller, who owned the exclusive Maxim's, had once run a saloon in the Lower East Side, where rowdy crowds had always loved singing waiters, such as Irving Berlin had once been. "'If customers from that joint could derive the utmost enjoyment from hearing waiters sing,' he saw no reason why "the more cultured people of 38th Street would not be similarly pleased with performances of higher quality."[3] Amid the plush décor of his new restaurant, Keller had singers and dancers entertain his patrons as they dined. The performers developed a new, more informal, and intimate style of delivery, mingling with the diners and even including them in their acts, blurring the line between performer and audience. Because city regulations required restaurant owners to purchase a theatrical license if they had a stage with scenery, the "show" emanated from the "floor."

Soon diners themselves took to the floor to dance. As the orchestra played, patrons tried out the new dances on the same floor where professional singers and dancers had just performed. When the city cracked down on these cabarets by imposing a 2:00 a.m. curfew, patrons simply signed membership cards to join a private "night club," which allowed them to go on dancing. Even more shocking to the guardians of morality was that people could also dance during the day at *thé dansants* (tea dances) that cabarets and hotels started as early as 2:00 p.m. and which extended into the once-sacred tea hour. (Tea, of course, was hardly the potable of such affairs; as one waiter remarked, "We seldom serve tea;—they wiggle much better on whisky."[4])

At such afternoon dances, one editorial moaned, "the young simply take advantage of the dance to embrace."[5] Particularly objectionable were such Latin imports as the tango, in which dancers pressed their bodies, upper *and* lower, together and even did a shocking "dip." Unescorted society ladies, married and unmarried, could learn these new steps from professional dancers who were barely a step above gigolos. In place of the traditional gypsy violins that played for listening, black bands now blared raucous ragtime music for dancing. "From the slum to the stage," intoned the *New York World* under the headline, "The City of Dreadful Dance": "from the stage to the restaurant, from restaurant to home, the dive dances have clutched and taken hold upon the young who know no better and the old who should."[6] So alarming was the dance craze that in 1913, a New York grand jury found "a presentment condemning the turkey trot and kindred dances and laying particular stress upon the fact that the hotels and cafés allow such dances in their establishments."[7]

The dance craze eventually was calmed by Irene and Vernon Castle, a young husband-and-wife team who did for the dance craze what "Alexander's Ragtime Band" had done for ragtime: they toned down the sensual and frenetic animal dances into refined romps that all could enjoy. Starting out by introducing such dances as the Turkey Trot and the Grizzly Bear in Parisian cabarets, the Castles developed an informally intimate style. They began their act by strolling to the dance floor from one of the tables, as if they were merely two customers getting up to dance. Their success in Paris brought invitations from New York, where they danced in Broadway shows, revues, and vaudeville. After their theatrical performances, they went to late-night, "roof-top" cabarets where they danced as part of the floor show.

The most enduring of their dances was the Fox Trot, which provided a four-beat alternative to the three-step waltz and the two-step of ragtime. The Fox Trot's alternation of slow gliding steps with quick ones opened up new possibilities for songwriters. As Mark Grant observes, "The foxtrot combines slow and fast, rhythmic flexibility and downbeat regularity, in a unique way. It can be made to swing or syncopate, yet it gives off a subtle lilt even when the rhythm is four-square and unswinging. It can be elegant and romantic or peppy and jazzy with a simple alteration of the basic tempo. It can be equally swank or earthy because it mixes courtly and folk dance elements in a way that no dance ever has."[8]

Irene Castle claimed that she and Vernon invented the Fox Trot in 1914. Originally, as David Jasen and Gene Jones observe, it was intended "mainly as a contrast to the flashier numbers that surrounded it. But, surprisingly audiences loved it.... The Fox Trot allowed couples less proficient than the Castles to learn it quickly and to improvise in the ballroom.... Within a few years of its introduction—and its identification with the Castles—the Fox Trot had become simply what one did when a ballad was played."[9]

As with every new craze, Tin Pan Alley was quick to exploit the popularity of dance. Catchy rhythm became all-important in songwriting. Music was conceived as an adjunct to dancing, rather than something merely to listen to, and lyrics were subservient to the musical beat. Many of the popular songs of the day had lyrics that simply "instructed" listeners in the new step (although the lyrical instructions were seldom complete and frequently carried suggestive overtones).

Once again, it was Irving Berlin who crystallized the new craze—and the sexual energy it evoked—in a song he wrote near the end of 1911, "Everybody's Doin' It Now." Setting the slangy catchphrase title to a sprightly, syncopated melody, Berlin again invited all to join in a joyous, infectious celebration. But where such an invitation in "Alexander's Ragtime Band" made the ragtime craze almost wholesome, in "Everybody's Doin' It Now" the singer urges an erotic abandon. Berlin's years of singing risqué parodies of popular songs in Chinatown saloons may have inspired him to insert the spoken repetitions of "Doin' it, Doin' it," to underscore the suggestive power of the simple verb (though, on the surface, what the lyric says they're "doin'" is a dance called the Grizzly Bear). The imagery of the lyric also depicts the collective loss of decorum on the dance floor and the new emphasis on bodily expression: a "ragtime couple" throw "their shoulders in the air," "snap their fingers," and exult, "It's a bear, it's a bear, it's a bear."

The same breakdown in propriety is mirrored in the grammar:

Ain't that music touching your heart?
Hear that trombone bustin' apart?

Such vernacular touches may have their roots in the dialect of coon songs, but here they are part of the new lingua franca of proper society casting off its genteel shackles. As "Everybody's Doin' It Now" became yet another of Irving Berlin's big hits, the songwriter reflected on his uncanny ability to capture a historical moment in song: "It was the dance craze put to music and words."[10]

The song also became a lightning rod for the defenders of morality, one of whom lamented of the whole dance craze, "Everybody's Overdoing It."[11] The New York Commission on Amusements and Vacation Resources for Working Girls, established in 1910, reported that "reckless and uncontrolled dances" were only "an opportunity for license and debauch." By 1912, the mayor of New York was pressured into imposing curfews on "so-called respectable places" that had been turned by the dance craze "into places of vulgarity if not infamy."[12] The mayor also promised an investigation of Tin Pan Alley firms such as Waterson, Berlin & Snyder, which had fueled the dance craze with risqué songs like "Everybody's Doin' It Now." The firm's pluggers were banned from some department stores, but still the dance craze rolled on. When Berlin himself performed the song at Hammerstein's Victoria Theatre, a newspaper reviewer described the kind of pandemonium that foreshadowed rock concerts:

> Everybody is doing it or doing something when this popular songwriter sings this ragtime classic.…The musicians in the orchestra begin swaying while playing their instruments, the curtain is raised and behind the scenes stage hands are discovered "doing it" with chairs, brooms, or whatever they may be handling when the strains of this contagious tune strikes them.[13]

EVERYBODY'S DOING IT NOW.

By IRVING BERLIN

Ain't the fun - ny strain   Go - in' to your brain?   Like   a   bot - tle of
Hon - ey, don't you smile,   Let   us rest   a while,   I'm   so weak in the

wine,   fine,   Hon', hon', hon', hon',   take   a   chance,
chest,   best,   Go,   go,   go,   go   get   a   chair,

One,   one,   one,   one   lit - tle   dance;   Can't you   see them all
No,   no,   no,   no,   leave   it   there;   Hon - ey,   if the mob

sway - ing up the hall?   Let's   be   get - tin'   in   line...............
still   are on the job,   I'm   as strong as   the   rest...............

CHORUS

Ev - 'ry-bo - dy's do - in' it, Do - in' it, do - in' it,

Ev - 'ry-bo - dy's do - in' it, Do - in' it, do - in' it, See that rag - time

cou - ple o - ver there, Watch them throw their shoul - ders in the air,

Snap their fin - gers, Hon - ey, I de - clare, It's a bear, it's a bear, it's a

Everybody's Doing It Now 4

bear.　There!　Ev -'ry-bo - dy's do - in' it, Do - in' it, do - in' it,

(Spoken)

(Spoken)

Ev -'ry-bo -dy's do-in' it, Do-in'it, do-in' it, Ain't that mu - sic touching your heart?

Hear that trombone bust-in' a - part? Come, come, come, come let us start,

Ev -'ry - bo - dy's do - in' it now...................................... now..............

Everybody's Doing It Now　4

Ernie Burnett

IN 1911, COMPOSER ERNIE BURNETT wrote a song with his wife, Maybelle, titled "Melancholy." Within the year, however, the Burnetts divorced, and in 1912, Ernie Burnett got another lyricist, George A. Norton, to rewrite the lyric as "My Melancholy Baby." The song was introduced at the Mozart Café in Denver, Colorado, by William Frawley, who many years later would play Fred Mertz on TV's *I Love Lucy*. (Frawley would go on to popularize other songs, such as "Carolina in the Morning" in 1922.)

In the days before radio's incessant playing of current hits quickly wore out a song's popularity, a song stayed popular for months, even years. "My Melancholy Baby" was still popular five years later in 1917 when Ernie Burnett went off to fight in World War I. During a battle in France, he was wounded, and, by the time medics found him, he had lost his memory. He had also lost his identifying "dog tags," so nobody knew who he was. He was placed in a field hospital, a total amnesiac, unable to communicate with anyone.

His dog tags were later found near the bodies of other soldiers, so the army assumed Ernie Burnett was dead. His name was put on the daily casualty list of soldiers wounded or killed in action. In the field hospital where Burnett lay comatose, a piano player came to entertain the wounded soldiers. He noticed Burnett's name on the daily casualty list and announced to the soldiers that the songwriter had been killed in action. He then played "My Melancholy Baby" in Burnett's memory.

When Ernie Burnett heard the melody, he sat up in bed and shouted, "I wrote that song!"—instantly, his memory returned.

"My Melancholy Baby" has gotten a bum rap. We've seen so many movies in which an inebriated bar patron yells to the piano player, "Play 'Melancholy Baby'" that many people think it's a sappy, sentimental song. But, as Alec Wilder notes, the melody is "good, containing highly unexpected phrases...unlike any other melody."[1] It adheres to nineteenth-century song patterns: the verse is just as long as the chorus (both sixteen bars). Lyrically, it has a casually conversational style established by its title, which sets the archly sophisticated "melancholy" against the slangy "baby." "My Melancholy Baby" was recorded by Bing Crosby and many other singers, and became a hit again in 1959 with a recording by Tommy Edwards. It's also been recorded by such jazz greats as Coleman Hawkins, Charlie Parker, Dizzy Gillespie, and Thelonious Monk.

2

My Melancholy Baby.

Words by
GEO. A. NORTON.

Music by
ERNIE BURNETT.

Moderato.

Come sweet-heart mine,   Dont sit and pine,   Tell me of the cares that make you
Birds in the trees,   Whis-per-ing breeze,   Should not fail to lul you in to

feel so blue.   What have I done?   An-swer me, Hon',
peace-ful dreams.   So tell me why   Sad-ly you sigh,

Have I ev-er said an un-kind word to you?   My love is true,
Sit-ting at the win-dow where the pale moon beams,   You should-n't grieve,

3

And just for you,
Try and be - lieve,

I'd do al-most an - y thing at an - y time,
Life is al-ways sun-shine when the heart beats true;

Dear, when you sigh
Be of good cheer,

Or when you cry,
Smile tho' you tears,

Some-thing seems to grip this ve - ry heart of mine.
When you're sad it makes me feel the same as you.

Chorus.

Come to me, my mel-an-chol-y ba - by,

Cud-dle up and don't be

blue;

All your fears are fool-ish fan-cy, may be,

My Melancholy Baby. 4

4

You know, dear, that I am strong for you. Ev'ry cloud must have a sil-ver

lin - ing, Wait un - til the sun shines through,

Smile my hon - ey dear, while I kiss a - way each tear, Or

else I shall be mel-an-chol- y too. Now won't you too._____

My Melancholy Baby. 4

Joseph McCarthy and James Monaco

IN 1913, COMPOSER James Monaco wrote a snappy, ragtime tune, and Joseph McCarthy took a vernacular catchphrase, "You made me do it," and gave it a romantic twist: "You made me...love you." He followed up with colloquial repetitions—"I didn't want to do it, I didn't want to do it" and "And all the time you knew it, I guess you always knew it." At the song's climactic moment, the repetitions become even more intense—and colloquial:

> Give me, give me what I cry for,
> You know you got the brand of kisses that I'd die for.

Lyrically and musically, "You Made Me Love You" was a fast-paced, jazzy number. But the performer who introduced it, Al Jolson, turned it into a slow, mournful lament. When he delivered the line "Give me, give me what I cry for," he made it even more colloquial by singing "Gimme, gimme what I cry for." He then underscored the plea by dropping to his knee. Jolson loved telling reporters that the gesture was spontaneous, caused by an ingrown toenail, but the knee-drop delivery had been used by other vaudeville performers.

In 1938, twenty-five years after Jolson had introduced "You Made Me Love You," the song launched Judy Garland's movie career. She had been signed by MGM on the basis of her stunning vocal talent, but Louis B. Mayer, MGM's studio head, worried that she was not attractive enough to be a star. (He affectionately referred to her as "My little hunchback.") But for the studio's celebration of Clark Gable's birthday, musical arranger Roger Edens adapted "You Made Me Love You" for Judy Garland to sing as an adolescent girl's fan letter to Gable. Edens wrote a special verse for Garland, beginning "Dear Mr. Gable, I am writing this to you…" He also toned down such passionate lyrics as "Give me, give me what I cry for" by substituting

I must tell you what I'm feeling,
The very mention of your name sets my heart reeling.

Finally, he added a monologue to register her crush on the star.

Garland's performance of "You Made Me Love You" at Gable's birthday party was so electrifying that Mayer had her reprise the number in *Broadway Melody of 1938*, where she played an adolescent girl smitten with Gable despite her mother, played by Sophie Tucker, warning her to stop worshipping movie stars. The success of Garland singing "You Made Me Love You" led to other parts in MGM movies, and, in the following year, to the lead in *The Wizard of Oz*—but only after MGM failed to sign Mayer's first choice for the role of Dorothy—Shirley Temple.

AL JOLSON'S TERRIFIC WINTER GARDEN HIT

YOU MADE ME LOVE YOU

I DIDN'T WANT TO DO IT

5

WORDS BY
JOE McCARTHY

MUSIC BY
JAMES V. MONACO

BROADWAY MUSIC CORPORATION
WILL VON TILZER PRESIDENT
145 WEST 45 ST ST. NEW YORK

2

"You Made Me Love You"

(I Did'nt Want To Do It)

Words by
JOE Mc CARTHY

Music by
JAMES V. MONACO

Moderato

I've been wor - ried all day long,—
I had pic - tured in my mind,—

Don't know if— I'm right or wrong,—
Some day I— would sure - ly find,—

I can't help— just what I say—
Some-one hand - some, some-one true,—

Your love makes me speak this way,— Why, oh! why should
But I nev - er thought of you,— Now my dream of

I feel blue,— Once I used to laugh at you,— But now I'm
love is o'er,— I want you and noth - ing more,— Come on, en-

cry - ing,— No use de - ny - ing,— There's no one else but you will do,—
fold me,— Come on and hold me— Just like you nev - er did be - fore,—

CHORUS

You made me love you, I did-n't want to do it   I did-n't want to do it,

p-f

4

You made me want you, And all the time you knew it I guess you al-ways knew it,

You made me hap-py some-times You made me glad ___

But there were times dear, You made me feel ___ so bad. ___

You made me sigh for I did-n't want to tell you I

You Made Me Love You - 4

5

did-n't want to tell you I want some love that's true, Yes I do, Deed I

do, You know I do. Give me give me what I cry for, You

know you got the brand of kiss - es that I'd die for You know you

made me love you. you.

You Made Me Love You - 4

W. C. Handy

AS A BOY, William Christopher Handy longed for a guitar—so that "I would be able to express the things I felt in sounds."[1] Guitars had only recently become affordable, and, as David Jasen and Gene Jones observe, soon "displaced the banjo as the poor man's instrument" and nurtured the development of the "blues":

> There was a musical as well as an economic reason for preferring the guitar. The hard sound of the banjo did not complement singing. The banjo was fine for clanging out a rhythm for dancing, but one had to sing over it rather than sing with it. The guitar's sound was softer and more flexible, and it allowed for subtlety and shading within a sung line. The guitar could practically sing back to the performer.[2]

Although many adults at the time could afford a guitar, a boy growing up in poverty had to save his pennies, earned from odd jobs, for months. When he was finally able to purchase a guitar, Handy held it up to his family and, at first, "was too full, too overjoyed" to speak. "'Look at it shine,' I said finally. 'It belongs to me—*me*. I saved up the money.'"

"My father was outraged...A guitar! 'One of the devil's playthings. Take it away. Take it away, I tell you...Take it back where it came from.'"[3]

Handy was forced to return the guitar in exchange for a dictionary, but his father, a preacher, did pay for organ lessons so his son could learn to play "sacred music."

When he was older, however, Handy bought a cornet, taught himself to play, and joined bands and vocal groups. Leaving home, he traveled in the South and Midwest, working as a day laborer, then joined the Mahara Minstrels. After touring with the black troupe, he was appointed the leader of one of its bands, replete with "a bright uniform, golden epaulets, and gleaming silk topper....

It was too good to be true."[4] Handy toured with his band for several years, and in 1900 played in Cuba, where he was intrigued by the rhythms of the tango and rumba.

In 1903, he accepted the position of leader of a band in Clarksdale, Mississippi, and here he steeped himself in what came to be called "blues." He had known such songs since he was a child growing up in Alabama. "In the Delta, however, I suddenly saw the songs with the eye of a budding composer."[5] Handy and his band moved on to Memphis where, in 1909, there was a three-way race for mayor. Handy was asked to compose a campaign song for one of the candidates, E. H. Crump. His tune "was the first of all the many published 'blues,' and it set a new fashion in American popular music and contributed to the rise of jazz, or, if you prefer, swing, and even boogie-woogie."[6]

After the election (which Crump won), Handy changed the tune to "Memphis Blues" and tried to get it published. When every music publisher he approached turned the song down, Handy decided to publish it himself. He paid a clerk at a Memphis department store to have a thousand copies of sheet music printed. As Handy waited for the printed sheet music to arrive from Cincinnati, Theron Bennett, a Denver music publisher, dropped by the department store and offered to be Handy's sales representative. As such, he promised to plug Handy's song all across the country just as he plugged his own firm's songs. Handy jumped at the chance for national distribution of "Memphis Blues."

Once the sheet music arrived, Handy watched as the clerk and Bennett set it up for sale on the counter in the department store. For the next few days, Handy kept checking with them about sales, but they told him customers found "Memphis Blues" too hard to play and, consequently, "there were practically no sales. It was hard to believe that Memphis, which loved its blues in the dance halls these two years, would now have none of it. But there lay the unsold copies as proof that my publishing venture was a failure."[7]

What Bennett and the clerk did not tell Handy was that they had initially ordered two thousand copies of "Memphis Blues" and that they were selling so quickly that they had ordered another thousand. Thus the "unsold" copies Handy saw on the shelves were the third thousand. Discouraged, he accepted Bennett's offer to buy out his copyright in "Memphis Blues." Bennett then had George Norton set a lyric to the tune. Norton's lyric only rubbed salt in Handy's wound because it celebrated Handy's own Memphis band. The song received many recordings, and the Castles used it to introduce the Fox Trot. "Memphis Blues" sold thousands of copies, but Handy received no royalties. Not until it was time to renew the copyright twenty-eight years later, did Handy reclaim what had been stolen from him.

Even though he would not learn until years later that he had been cheated, Handy saw the success of "Memphis Blues" and vowed that from then on he would publish his own songs. Determined to write another blues, he checked into a hotel room to concentrate apart from his four rambunctious children.

Working through the night, he took inspiration from his memory of being in St. Louis years before: "broke, unshaven, wanting even a decent meal, and standing before the lighted saloon in St. Louis without a shirt under my frayed coat." From that evening came another memory that at the time seemed unimportant: "I had seen a woman whose pain seemed even greater. She had tried to take the edge off her grief by heavy drinking, but it hadn't worked. Stumbling along the poorly lighted street, she muttered as she walked, 'My man's got a heart like a rock cast in the sea,' " a line Handy incorporated into the refrain of "St. Louis Blues."[8]

After thinking about his song through the night, Handy finally put it down on paper. He wrote, "I hate to see that evening sun go down," reflecting, "if you ever had to sleep on the cobbles down by the river in St. Louis, you'll understand that complaint."[9] As he developed the song, Handy followed the AAB pattern of twelve-bar blues, where an initial four-bar A-phrase,

(A) I hate to see de evening sun go down

is repeated, with a slight variation, musically and lyrically:

(A') Hate to see de evenin' sun go down

Then a third four-bar phrase, the B-phrase, varies and completes the musical and lyrical idea:

(B) Cause ma baby, he done lef' dis town

He also used the "flat thirds and sevenths (now called 'blue notes') although its prevailing key was the major."[10]

In other sections of the song, however, Handy broke into a tango rhythm. The tango was one of the most popular dances of the dance craze, and Handy believed it was based on the African *tangana* that Moors brought to Spain and then black slaves carried to America.

St. Louis 'oman
Wid her diamon' rings
Pulls dat man roun'
By her apron strings.
'Twan't for powder
An' for store-bought hair
De man ah love
Would not gone nowhere.

Here the singer laments that her lover pursues a St. Louis woman who "whitens" herself with powder and a wig, but the singer loves her man for his very blackness:

Blackest man in de whole St. Louis,
Blacker de berry, sweeter are the juice.

By the time he completed the song, it was time to join his band for the evening dance. When they played "St. Louis Blues," despite its unusual form, the dancers "seemed electrified."[11] Handy invited the band back to his home to celebrate his success, only to find he had forgotten to tell his wife that he had checked into a hotel the night before to work on a song.

"St. Louis Blues" was an enormous success that established W.C. Handy on Tin Pan Alley, opened the door for black performers, and brought the blues into America's cultural mainstream.

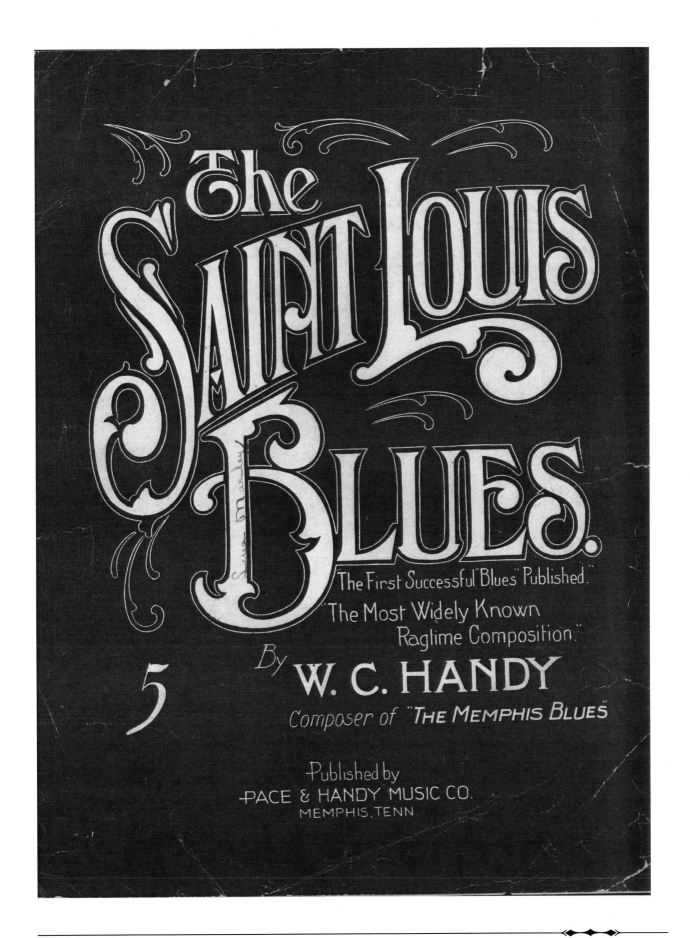

Respectfully Dedicated To Mr. Russell Gardiner.
"The Banner Buggy Man"

The "St. Louis Blues"

W. C. HANDY

I hate to see de eve-ning sun go down _____ Hate to see
Been to de Gypsy to get ma for-tune tole _____ To de Gypsy
You ought to see dat stove pipe brown of mine _____ Lak he owns

de evenin' sun go down _____ Cause ma ba - by he done lef dis
done got ma for-tune tole _____ Cause Im is wile bout ma Jel-ly
de Di-mon Jo-seph line _____ He'd make a cross-eyed 'o-man go stone

town. _____   Feel - in' to - mor - row   lak   ah feel to -
Roll. _____   Gyp - sy done tole   me   "don't   you wear no
blin'. _____   Black-er than mid - night   teeth   lak flags o'

day _____   Feel to - mor - row   lak ah feel to - day _____
black _____   Yas she done tole me   "don't you wear no   black_____
truce _____   Black - est   man   in de whole St   Louis, _____

_____   I'll pack my trunk   make ma git a - way _____   St. Lou-is
_____   Go to St Louis   you can win him back _____   Help me to
_____   Black-er de ber - ry,   sweet - er are the   juice _____   A - bout a

8va ad lib.

The St. L. B. 4

4

'o - man   wid   her dia-mon'   rings _____ Pulls dat man roun'
Cai - ro   make St Louis by ma - self _____ Git to Cai - ro
crap game   he knows a pow'-ful   lot _____ But when work-time comes,

by her a-pron   strings _____   'Twant for pow-der   an' for store-bought
find ma ole friend Jeff _____   Gwine to pin ma -   - self close to his
he's on de   dot _____   Gwine to ask him   for a cold ten -

hair _____   De   man ah love   would not gone no - where. ___
side _____   If   ah flag his train   I   sho can   ride. ___
spot _____   What it takes to git it he's cer-t'n - ly got. ___

The St. L. B. 4

108

CHORUS

Melody from "The Jogo Blues"

Got de St Louis Blues jes blue as ah can be
I loves dat man lak a school-boy loves his pie

Dat man got a heart lak a rock cast in the sea
Lak a Ken-tuck-y Col'-nel loves his mint an rye,

Or else he would-n't gone
I'll love ma ba-by till

1. *Spoken* *2.* *D.C.*

so far from me. Dog-gone-it! me
de day ah die. die

The St. L.B. 4

Jerome Kern

<figure>◆◆◆</figure>

IN ADDITION TO PLUGGING its wares in vaudeville, Tin Pan Alley managed to get its songs into Broadway musicals as "interpolations"—songs added to the score of a musical by lyricists and composers other than the writers of the original score. As we read in the chapter on Charles K. Harris, "After the Ball" was interpolated into the score of *A Trip to Chinatown* when it was on the road in Milwaukee. Interpolations kept a show fresh, and gave an American touch to the many musicals that were imported from Britain in the wake of the enormous success of Gilbert and Sullivan's *H.M.S. Pinafore* after its authorized premiere in America in 1879 (a year after it opened in London).

Jerome Kern broke into Broadway by writing interpolations, such as "How'd You Like to Spoon with Me?" for *The Earl and the Girl* (1905). Then in 1907, Franz Lehar's *The Merry Widow* emigrated from Austria to America and rekindled the American love for operetta—and the waltz. It was followed by other imports as well as American imitations such as Victor Herbert's *Naughty Marietta* (1911). As Lee Davis observes of the renewed interest in Viennese operetta, "The limited-range, almost spoken melodies that characterized British musical theatre gave way to full range, sustained melody lines.... Opulence was the operative word. Ninety-member choruses, forty-five piece orchestras, five-act operettas."[1] But a composer such as Kern could write interpolations in either the light British or heavy Viennese style—always with an American touch.

Kern got an opportunity to write more than interpolations when Lee and Jake Shubert planned a spectacular show for the opening of their new Winter Garden theater in 1911. The Shuberts asked Kern to write most of the songs for the show, and one of his songs, "Paris Is a Paradise for Coons," was given a stunning performance by a young singer in blackface named Al Jolson.

When producer Charles Froman asked him to contribute four interpolated songs to *The Girl from Utah*, Kern demanded that his name be listed in the billing for the show's score. One of his interpolations, "They Didn't Believe Me," has become one of the great standards in *The American Song Book*. As songwriter Alec Wilder observed, the song "was a definite departure from all the songs which preceded it. Outside of its un-Viennese freshness…the melodic line of 'They Didn't Believe Me' is as natural as walking. Yet its form is not conventional even by the standards of that time.…It is evocative, tender, strong, shapely, and like all good creations which require time for their expression, has a beginning, middle, and end."[2]

The lyric by Michael Rourke, writing under the pen name of Herbert Reynolds, skillfully weaves a romantic idea around the catchphrase title, shifting from "They Didn't Believe Me" to "They'll never believe me" when the singer's beloved accepts his proposal. A problem arose when Kern threw a triplet into the melody, and Rourke came up with the phrase "And I cert'n-ly am goin' to tell them," forcing "cert'n-ly-am" to be sung in three syllables to fit the triplet. Singers have long since overcome that awkwardness by using a contraction: "And I'm certainly going to tell them" so that the three syllables of "cer-tain-ly" are sung over the triplet. The contraction "I'm" also gave the song a casually conversational feel that was a welcome American touch at a time when florid operetta songs were dominating Broadway.

"They Didn't Believe Me" remained popular for several months, reaching the Top Twenty in January of 1916 and remaining there through May. Gerald Bordman notes that "Historians generally agree that the song established the modern ballad—the $\frac{4}{4}$ time song—as we still know it today and allowed it to replace the waltz as the principal song in contemporary musical comedy."[3] When young George Gershwin heard "They Didn't Believe Me" played at a wedding, he quit his job as a song plugger on Tin Pan Alley to go to work on Broadway as a rehearsal pianist. Kern's song made him realize that music written for Broadway shows could be artistically superior—yet still as popular—as songs that emanated from the assembly lines of Tin Pan Alley.

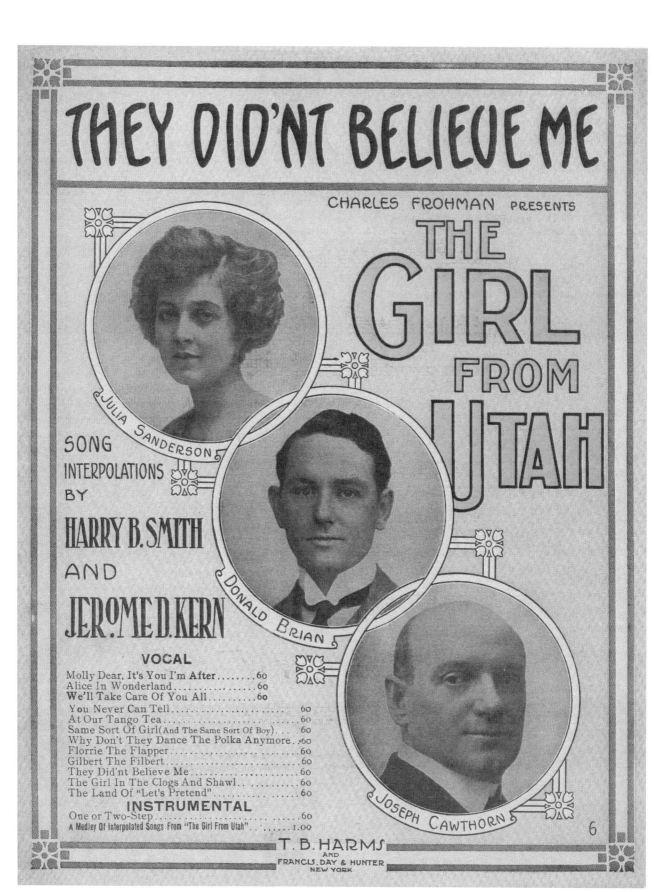

They Didn't Believe Me.

Words by
HERBERT REYNOLDS

Music by
JEROME KERN.

5050 - 4

114

4

They did-n't be - lieve me! _____ They did-n't be - lieve me ___
They did-n't be - lieve me! _____ They did-n't be - lieve me ___

_ Your lips, your eyes, your cheeks, your hair are in a
_ Your lips, your eyes, your cur - ly hair are in a

class be - yond com - pare You're the lov - li - est girl _____
class be - yond com - pare You're the lov - li - est thing _____

_ that one could see! _____ And when I tell them ___
_ that one could see! _____ And when I tell them ___

ASCAP

IN 1913, COMPOSER Victor Herbert met with eight other men in the music business to discuss a problem. Ironically, the men met at Luchow's restaurant on Union Square—one of the restaurants that was causing the problem. Like many other restaurants, Luchow's entertained diners by playing popular songs of the day but without paying any compensation to the songwriters or their publishers. People could sit in Luchow's and hear the same songs from a Victor Herbert show—free—for which they would have to buy a ticket to hear in the theater. The nine men decided to create an organization similar to the French SACEM (Société des auteurs, compositeurs et éditeurs de musique), which, since 1871, had been collecting fees for public performances of songs by European composers, lyricists, and publishers.

On February 13, 1914, the men met again with more than one hundred other songwriters to form ASCAP, an acronym for the American Society of Composers, Authors (lyricists), and Publishers. ASCAP sold licenses to restaurants, cabarets, and other businesses that allowed them to perform songs written and published by ASCAP members; ASCAP then distributed the money it received from license fees back to its members.

Initially, restaurants scoffed when ASCAP told them they would have to purchase licenses to perform songs they had until then been playing for free. They even told the songwriters they should be grateful that restaurants and cabarets were "plugging" their songs and boosting sheet-music sales. The issue went to court when Herbert's publisher, G. Schirmer Music, sued Shanley's restaurant for performing Herbert's song "Sweethearts" without authorization. Lawyers for Shanley's argued that it was a restaurant, not a theater, and that songs were performed only incidentally to the serving of food. Nathan Burkan, the young attorney who had helped songwriters such as Charles K. Harris get Congress to pass a new copyright bill in 1909, skillfully represented the fledgling ASCAP.

In a decision that came from the United States Supreme Court, Justice Oliver Wendell Holmes ruled that Shanley's was performing songs in order to attract customers. "If the music did not pay," he wrote, "it would be given up."[1] Even though tickets were not sold at the door of the restaurant, Holmes ruled that the unlicensed use of songs was an infringement of copyright.

With that ruling, any use of ASCAP songs earned profits for songwriters that would supplement and sometimes even outweigh the royalties that came from sheet-music and record sales. Initially spreading $24,000 in royalty fees among its members, ASCAP could not pay its first dividends until 1921; by 1950 it was doling out between $15 and $16 million a year to its members, who still had to pay only ten dollars a year as a membership fee. Irving Berlin, even though he was not one of the founding members of ASCAP, was one of its most ardent supporters. He would stop a fellow songwriter on the street to borrow ten dollars then shake his friend's hand and say, "Congratulations, you're now a member of ASCAP." With the establishment of ASCAP, as long as their songs were still under copyright, songwriters received an income when the songs were performed.

Irving Berlin on Broadway

WHILE JEROME KERN MOVED up on Broadway by writing interpolated songs for musical shows, Irving Berlin, despite inserting a few of his songs into Broadway musicals, remained fixed on Tin Pan Alley. In 1914, however, after the success of "Alexander's Ragtime Band," Broadway producer Charles Dillingham invited Berlin to write the score for a new musical comedy, *Watch Your Step*. Berlin recognized that the invitation represented "the first time Tin Pan Alley got into the legitimate theater."[1] Up until then, Broadway scores had been created by trained composers, such as Victor Herbert, rather than the largely untrained tunesmiths, such as Berlin himself, who cranked out songs for Tin Pan Alley. As Larry Stempel notes, "Berlin's achievement represented the first time an Alley songsmith with no connection to the stage other than as another outlet for his work provided an entire evening's worth of songs for what was essentially a book show, perhaps even a musical comedy."[2]

Berlin would be working with the eminent librettist Harry B. Smith, who had written more than three hundred "books" for Broadway musicals, many of which were simply adaptations of older plays. For *Watch Your Step*, Smith recycled an old French play about heirs to a fortune who have to compete for the $2 million legacy by adhering to the stipulation that they *not* fall in love. Given that story line, Irving Berlin now had to do something he had never done on Tin Pan Alley—integrate his songs into dramatic situations and tailor them to specific characters. Though far from the kind of complete integration of song and story that would sweep Broadway in the 1940s after Rodgers and Hammerstein's *Oklahoma!*, Berlin's songs for *Watch Your Step* grew out of Smith's libretto, and Smith also wrote portions of the story to fit Berlin's songs. As a librettist, Harry

Smith would normally write song lyrics as well as dialogue, but Berlin wanted to continue his usual fashion of writing both lyrics and music for his songs. Berlin acknowledged that Smith "was a great versifier and I was a little insecure about my lyrics. So I said to him, 'If you want me to redo my lyrics, go ahead.' And he said, 'Irving, don't ever let anyone touch your lyrics.'"[3]

Watch Your Step featured Vernon and Irene Castle. In uniting the Castles with Berlin, Dillingham shrewdly cashed in on the very people who had brought ragtime and the dancing craze into respectability. The musical opened to critical and popular raves. The lion's share of the credit went to Berlin's score, which featured songs more complex than anything he had written before. Several songs shifted between major and minor keys, sometimes in the space of a few bars. In "Ragtime Opera Medley," he created a musical collage out of several operas—*Faust, Carmen, La Bohème, Madame Butterfly, Pagliacci, Aida*—in a scene where the ghost of Verdi pleads, in a sequence of songs based on *Rigoletto*: "Please don't rag my melody—let my *Rigoletto* be." These songs were so closely tied to the story and characters of *Watch Your Step* that most did not go on to become independently popular.

Except for one—Berlin's first "counterpoint" song. Always alert to the current musical fashion, Berlin juxtaposed the sentimental ballads of the 1890s with the new rage for ragtime. In a contrapuntal duet, he has one singer plead for a simple melody "like my mother sang to me," while the other singer wants to change that "classical nag" to "some sweet beautiful drag." As other characters join in the debate, the audience realizes that the two melodies and lyrics fit together perfectly. Berlin was cavalier about bringing off such a tour de force, saying "the musical part didn't give me any trouble" but "the difficulty was getting two lyrics so that they didn't bump into each other."[4]

"(Play a) Simple Melody" was popular in 1914, but in 1950 it was revived in a recording by Bing Crosby and his son Gary that stayed on *Your Hit Parade* for eleven weeks.

Berlin's achievement in writing his first Broadway score was recognized by the critics:

> Irving Berlin stands out like the Times building does in the Square. That youthful marvel of syncopated melody is proving things in "Watch Your Step," firstly that he is not alone a rag composer, and that he is one of the greatest lyrical writers America has ever produced.[5]

Berlin always maintained that the opening night of *Watch Your Step* had been the greatest thrill of his life. He spent it with his mother and sisters in the audience. He had long before reestablished relations with his family after having run away from home and had moved his mother out of the Lower East Side to her own house in the Bronx. With her limited English, Lena Baline could barely follow the lyrics to his songs, but she must have glowed when she saw her Izzy, in response to cries for "Composer! Composer!!" at the end of the performance, take to the stage, bow, and offer a few nervous words of thanks. After the show, he dutifully escorted her home then returned to his apartment to await what turned out to be smashing reviews.

Watch Your Step was a genuinely American musical that challenged European operetta as powerfully as had the shows of George M. Cohan a decade earlier. Victor Herbert saw the influence of Tin Pan Alley on American musical theater as a major shift from songs that were integral to story and character, to songs that could achieve independent popularity through sheet-music and record sales:

> They must have words that are independent of the play—that is, on some general theme and attractive to the person who has not seen the play. I think that this may have had its effect in weaning us away from comic opera in which lyrics are woven into the plot and are part of it.[6]

The fact that *Watch Your Step* premiered in the first Broadway season after the outbreak of World War I fueled its success. American audiences now wanted to embrace native rather than Germanic and Viennese fare. "While the war was going on, operetta fell into disfavor with the majority of producing managers," noted Harry B. Smith. "The Teutonic operetta crop failed."[7]

Simple Melody

Ernesta, Algy and Chorus

Words and Music
by IRVING BERLIN

Simple Melody. 3

When Irving Berlin worked as a singing waiter in the Pelham Café in Chinatown, he taught himself to play on the saloon's piano. Like many self-taught pianists, Berlin gravitated to the black keys, so that the only key he could play in was F-sharp. "The black keys are right there under your fingers," he said, "Children who learn to play instinctively always learn the key of F-sharp," while "the key of C is for people who study music."[8]

He was able to transcend the limitations of that key by purchasing a "transposing piano," which had a lever that allowed the pianist to continue playing in the one key he knew but hear how the music sounded in other keys. A step up from the player piano, a transposing piano could be purchased from the Weser Company for $100. Berlin called the transposing piano his "Buick," and it traveled with him wherever he went. It now sits in the Smithsonian Institution.

For most of his life, Berlin's other musical limitation was that he could not read music. He hired various musical "secretaries," who could take down his melodies in musical notation, including picking out the harmonies, which Berlin could *hear*, chord by chord, in his musical ear but could not play.

In a paean to his "Buick," "I Love a Piano," Berlin again proved himself the "ragged meter man" by creating clever mismatches between lyrics and music. He crunched the three syllables of "pee-a-no" into the slangy two syllables of "pyan-o" to fit two musical notes (though singers have frequently missed the point, singing, more archly, "on a pee-a-no" rather than the vernacular "up-on a pyan-o." Perhaps drawing on the risqué parodies of popular songs he'd sung at the Pelham Café, he turned piano-playing into an erotic encounter:

> *I love to run my fingers o'er the keys—the ivories.*
> *And with the peddle, I love to meddle.*

The clever internal rhymes—"*o'er* the keys—the i-*vor*-ies" drive the lyric forward to register the performer's exuberance. The metaphoric connection between a piano and a woman transforms the cliché "a fine way to treat a lady" into "I know a fine way to treat a Steinway." He also juxtaposes the genteel "high-toned" piano/lady against the more sensuous "baby grand."

At the climax of the song, he passionately spells out the name of his beloved instrument:

> *Give me a P-I-A-N-O, Oh, Oh, Oh*

"I Love a Piano" was featured in *Stop! Look! Listen!*, Berlin's second complete Broadway score, where it was lavishly staged with six pianos on a set that resembled an enormous keyboard.

Although Berlin was now writing Broadway scores, Alec Wilder finds "no theatrical flavor" in "I Love a Piano," nor other songs from *Watch Your Step*. "The pop writer aspect of Berlin's talent was still predominant."[9]

I LOVE A PIANO
CHAS. B. DILLINGHAM presents
GABY DESLYS
In a new "Musical Comedy"
STOP! LOOK! LISTEN!
THAT HULA HULA . . $ .60
I LOVE A PIANO 60
THE GIRL ON THE MAGAZINE 60
EVERYTHING in AMERICA IS RAGTIME . . .60
WHEN I GET BACK TO THE U. S. A. 60
STOP, LOOK, LISTEN . .60
TEACH ME HOW TO LOVE 60
FATHER WANTED ME to LEARN A TRADE .60
BLOW YOUR HORN . . .60
SAILOR SONG 60
I LOVE TO DANCE 60
WHEN I'M OUT WITH YOU 60
THE LAW MUST BE OBEYED 60
SELECTION 1.00
BOOK BY
HARRY B. SMITH
STAGED BY
R. H. BURNSIDE
LYRICS & MUSIC
· BY ·
IRVING BERLIN
PUBLISHED BY
IRVING BERLIN INC.
Nº 1571 B'WAY NEW YORK
BARBELLE

I LOVE A PIANO

by IRVING BERLIN

nets were my pets, and a slide trom-bone I thought was sim-ply di-
lude to the crude lit-tle par-ty sing-er, who don't know when to

vine.___ But to-day, when they play, I could hiss them; Ev-'ry
pause.___ At her best I de-test the so-pran-o, But I

bar is a jar to my sys-tem; But there's one
run to the one at the pian-o, I al-ways

mu-si-cal in-stru-ment, that I call mine.___
love the ac-comp-ni-ment and that's be-cause: ___

Spencer Williams

SPENCER WILLIAMS'S MOTHER was a prostitute who, along with her sister, ran a bordello on Basin Street in New Orleans. When his mother died, the sister raised the boy until he was a teenager, when he was sent off to relatives in Birmingham. By then, however, Spencer had absorbed the "rocking New Orleans sound" and learned to play piano himself.[1] In 1907, he quit school and headed for Chicago, where he got a job as a piano player in an amusement park. There he started writing songs and managed to place a few with music publishers.

In 1915, he wrote a song called "I Ain't Got Nobody Much," a title very similar to a song from 1914 called 'I Ain't Got Nobody." A publisher bought Williams's song in 1916, but when he heard about the earlier "I Ain't Got Nobody," he bought that song too. The publisher then brought out both songs with a cover depicting Sophie Tucker and Bert Williams (the latter probably because his signature piece was a song called "Nobody" from 1905). It was Spencer Williams's version of "I Ain't Got Nobody," with a lyric by Roger Graham, that became a hit, placing in the Top Ten from January through May 1917.

According to David Jasen and Lee Jones, the chorus of both songs starts out with "the famous wailing fifth and the three descending chromatic notes ('I_____ ain't got no...'), but then Williams's melody "syncopates by putting a rest on the first beat of measure three. The remainder of the Williams chorus is spiked with syncopations,"[2] probably the influence of the ragtime he heard growing up in New Orleans. "Spencer Williams's career obviously began with a petty theft, but his reworking of the purloined song earned its staying power."[3]

I AIN'T GOT NOBODY

MUCH
AND NOBODY CARES FOR ME

FEATURED BY
Paul Biese and His Novelty Orchestra
AT THE
NEW BISMARCK GARDEN, CHICAGO.

SOPHIE TUCKER

VICTOR
RECORD
No 18133

LYRIC BY
ROGER GRAHAM
MUSIC BY
SPENCER WILLIAMS

Frank K. Root & Co.
CHICAGO — NEW YORK

Albert & Son, Australasian Agents, Sydney, Australia.

I AIN'T GOT NOBODY MUCH

Words by
ROGER GRAHAM.

Music by
SPENCER WILLIAMS.

Slow Drag

There's a say - ing go - ing 'round, And I be - gin to think it's
If I on - ly had some - one That I could on - ly call my

true, ____ It's aw - ful hard to love some - one When
own, ____ For I would mar - ry them at once And

I Ain't Got Nobody Much 4

135

no - bod - y cares for me. (I got the Blues, The Weary Blues)

And _____ I'm sad and lone - ly,

Won't some - bod - y come and take a chance with me? _____

I'll sing sweet love songs, hon - ey, all the

I Ain't Got Nobody Much. 4

I Ain't Got Nobody Much 4

George M. Cohan Goes to War

ALTHOUGH GEORGE M. COHAN had a flurry of hits in the early years of the twentieth century, his success waned by the end of the first decade. Still, in 1917, when President Woodrow Wilson signed the declaration that plunged the United States into World War I, Cohan's patriotic spirit was roused. Shutting himself up in his study for almost two days, he finally emerged with a song. As his daughter Mary recalled, he called the family into the living room. "We all sat down and waited expectantly because we loved to hear him sing. He put a big tin pan on his head, used a broom for his gun on his shoulder, and he started to mark time like a soldier."[1] As he sang "Johnnie get your gun, get your gun, get your gun," he marched around the room. With its infectious, repetitive musical and lyrical phrases, the song expresses rousing determination, especially in its concluding line with its clever twist on the title: "And we won't come back till it's over—over there."

Despite a deluge of other wartime songs, from the dovish "I Didn't Raise My Boy to Be a Soldier" to the hawkish "I Didn't Raise My Boy to Be a Coward," Cohan's "Over There" became the martial anthem of the country. Sheet-music sales quickly climbed into the millions. Nora Bayes recorded it and featured it in her vaudeville act. Enrico Caruso also made a recording with choruses in English and French. "Over There" was the number one song from September 1917 through January 1918, not slipping to the number two spot until February of that year. Though it would be his last hit song in a career that would continue for more than twenty years, "Over There" is the consummate expression of Cohan's flag-waving patriotism.

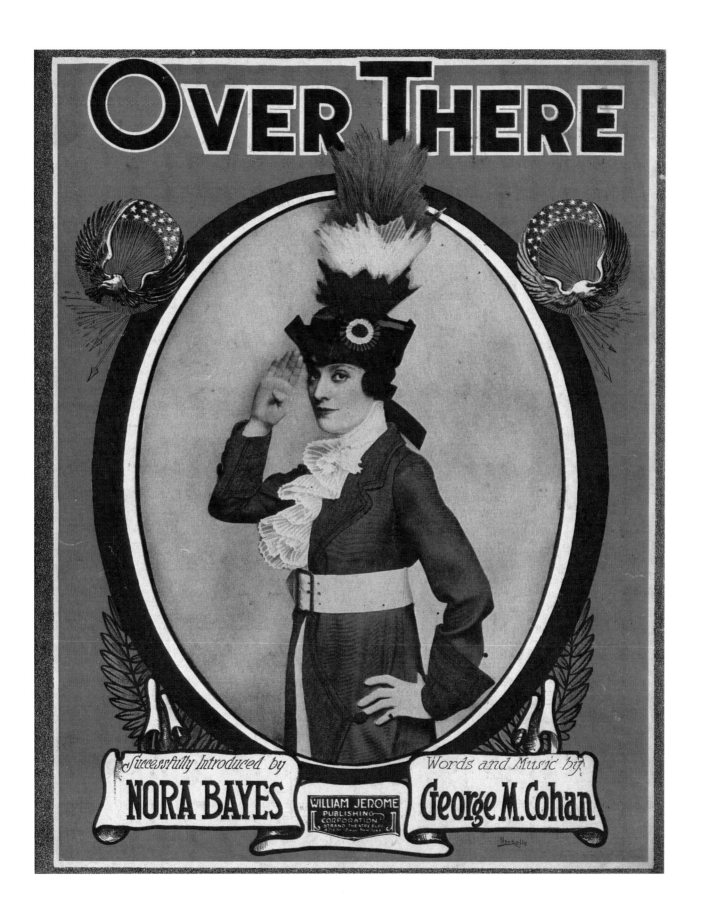

OVER THERE.

All performing and mechanical
rights reserved by the publishers

By GEORGE M. COHAN.

Refrain.

O - ver there _____ o - ver there _____ Send the word, send the word o - ver

there _____ That the Yanks are com - ing the Yanks are com - ing The drums rum -

tum-ming ev'- ry - where _____ So pre - pare _____ say a pray'r _____ Send the

word, send the word to be - ware _____ We'll be o - ver we're com-ing o -

ver And we won't come back till it's o-ver o - ver there. O - ver there.

Over There

F.J.LAWSON CO.N.Y.

The Princess Shows

This is the trio of musical fame,
  Bolton and Wodehouse and Kern:
Better than anyone else you can name,
  Bolton and Wodehouse and Kern.
Nobody knows what on earth they've been bitten by,
  All I can say is I mean to get lit an' buy
Orchestra seats for the next one that's written by
  Bolton and Wodehouse and Kern[1]

THE PRINCESS THEATRE THAT once stood at 104 West 39th Street had an auditorium that held only 299 seats ("since a number of stringent laws applied to any theatre seating three hundred or more"[2]). Given its size, roughly a fifth of the number of seats in most Broadway theaters, the Princess was ideally suited to intimate musicals that differed markedly from the bloated operettas that lined Broadway. The so-called Princess shows would have only two acts instead of operetta's usual five. Concomitantly, they would usually have only two sets as opposed to the dozen or more in operetta. Where operettas had an orchestra of forty musicians and a chorus upwards of ninety, Princess shows had only eleven musicians and a chorus of between eight and twelve singers. Set in contemporary America, Princess shows required only simple, everyday costumes rather than the elaborate regalia of operetta. "The performers would be young, so that their agents wouldn't be too obnoxious; and the composers and librettists would be fairly unknown, so that their financial demands wouldn't be too demanding."[3]

By the time of the Princess shows (ca. 1915), American musicals also featured a tap-dancing chorus. As Gerald Bordman observes, "Tap dancing was introduced in 1903 but was employed only by soloists for the most part. It took several years before choreographers caught on to its electrifying effect when performed by choruses. Ballet, when used at all, was the province of operetta, not musical comedy."[4]

The visionary who saw that the small theater could spawn a new kind of musical was Bessie Marbury, who had done much to publicize the Castles and the Dance Craze. She persuaded Ray Comstock, who managed the Princess Theatre for the Shubert brothers, that simple, streamlined productions could be mounted for as little as $7,500. Marbury and Comstock brought in composer and playwright Paul Rubens for their first show, but it quickly became apparent that Rubens was not up to the music or the libretto. Marbury then sought out Jerome Kern to bolster the music, and Kern suggested she also take on a young playwright, Guy Bolton. In Bolton, Kern had found someone who could integrate a song into story and characters, so that music flowed seamlessly out of—and back into—dialogue. After years of seeing his interpolated songs shoehorned into shows, Kern was certain that with Guy Bolton he could fuse music, dialogue, and song lyrics.

When he mentioned Bolton's name to Marbury, she said. "Oh yes. I know his work. He shows promise."

"And now," Kern supposedly said, "You're going to promise him shows."[5]

The first of the Princess shows was *Nobody Home*. It opened on April 20, 1915, and proved so successful that Comstock moved it to a bigger theater where it could accommodate larger audiences. Still, the model was set for Princess shows—small, sophisticated, witty, contemporary musicals that would move American musical theater away from operetta to something new—American musical comedy.

The most successful of the Princess shows was *Oh, Boy!* in 1917. Lee Davis remarks:

> There had never been ... a show so chic, so up to date, so unfailingly tuneful, so unflaggingly funny, and so deliciously clever ... both public and critics threw their collective hats in the air. It was the biggest hit the Princess would ever have, and in retrospect and reality, it was the supreme Princess show. Nothing Guy and Jerry had written for the Princess before matched it; nothing they would write for the Princess after would equal its success. It was their watershed. And so, it became a watershed for the American musical theatre.[6]

The public's embrace of the Princess shows was part of a deepening revulsion against things German and Austrian—including operetta—after America's entry into World War I. The war stemmed the flow of new operettas, but even production of existing operettas would not only supply funds to Germany and Austro-Hungary in the form of royalties but would give them cultural prestige. "Other wars 'went no deeper than the physical aspects,' remarked one of President

Wilson's spokesmen, 'but German 'Kultur' raised issues that had to be fought out in the hearts and minds of the people as well as on the actual firing line.'"[7]

The Princess shows also marked another, more gradual cultural change. Ever since the creation of film, movies had lured away "less affluent, less educated playgoers"—especially silent films, which appealed to the waves of new immigrants, since they required little knowledge of English to follow the story. "The theatre," observes Gerald Bordman, "was slowly, subtly becoming more elitist—perhaps in the best sense of the word—and the Princess, with its meager balcony, was more elitist still."[8]

To be sure, several of the Princess shows," such as Kern and Wodehouse's *Have a Heart* and *Leave It to Jane*, did not even open at the Princess Theatre, and those that did quickly moved on to larger houses where they could draw considerably more box-office revenue. Still, the size of the Princess and its paucity of cheap seats, marked a change in the nature of the Broadway theater audience. The trade-off was that Broadway productions could provide increasingly sophisticated fare, particularly in the song lyrics for musicals.

P. G. Wodehouse

BY THE TIME THEY wrote *Oh, Boy!* Guy Bolton and Jerome Kern had added a third collaborator to become a triumvirate. The lyrics for the first of the Princess shows, *Nobody Home*, were written by Schuyler Greene, a seasoned Tin Pan Alley lyricist but not at the innovative level of Jerome Kern and Guy Bolton. He lacked what Bessie Marbury called the "Princess touch—that sense of where to stop the talking and begin the singing and the ability to create effortless, clever, sophisticated *fun* onstage."[1]

The Princess touch in lyrics materialized when P. G. Wodehouse joined the team. Pelham Grenville Wodehouse, British-born like Guy Bolton, was writing for magazines such as *Vanity Fair* in England and the *Saturday Evening Post* in America, including stories about a butler named Jeeves who takes care of his eccentric young master, Bertie Wooster. Kern had worked with "Plum" (as Wodehouse was known) on shows in England and saw him as a potential lyricist. Guy Bolton was an excellent comic playwright and a master of one-liners:

"I've got money to burn."

"Well, you've met your match."[2]

But Bolton also made sure his jokes grew out of character and situation.

Still, the art of writing lyrics was a very different endeavor and needed a specialist. Wodehouse was open to the idea of joining the team, but his idea of writing lyrics was based on Gilbert and Sullivan's operettas, in which the lyrics were written first. Gilbert essentially wrote light verse poems, similar to his collection of *Bab Ballads*, and Sullivan set them to music. Over time, Gilbert learned to make his light verse more "singable" by providing long vowels and liquid and nasal consonants, but still his words came first. In American songwriting, though, it was usually the music that came first as Wodehouse soon learned.

When Wodehouse agreed to "have a go" at this American way of songwriting, he made a delightful discovery. Citing one instance of how Kern's sequence of "twiddly little notes" inspired him to come up with a subtle internal rhyme in the phrase "If every day you *bring* her diamonds and pearls on a *string*," Wodehouse said, "I couldn't have thought of that, if I had done the lyric first, in a million years. Why, dash it, it doesn't *scan*."[3] What Wodehouse meant was that Gilbert's lyrics had the metrically regular *scansion* of light verse:

> When I **mere**-/ ly from him/ **part**-ed,
> > We were **near**-/ly **bro**-ken/ **heart**-ed.
> When in **se**-/quell **re**-u-/**ni**-ted,
> > We were **e**-/qual-ly/de-**light**-ed.

Wodehouse discovered—and revealed to aspiring lyricists—that you could turn the liabilities of popular songwriting into an asset. By letting the music come first, you could rhyme in clever ways without departing from colloquial phrasing. With the music—rather than a poetic meter—setting the rhythm, song lyrics could sound perfectly conversational yet have clever rhymes. In a song such as "Cleopatterer," witty rhymes emerge from colloquial phrasing:

> At dancing Cleopatterer
> Was always on the spot.
> She gave those poor Egyptian ginks
> Something else to watch besides the sphinx.

Following the music forced a lyricist to be conversational. When Kern put a triplet in the middle of a musical phrase in the song "Bill," Wodehouse used the three notes for a casual interjection that sidesteps sentimentality: "I love him because he's—*I don't know*—because he's just my Bill."

Wodehouse also integrated the light-verse wit of his lyrics into character and dramatic situation. In *Oh, Boy!* he gave the formulaic love song a new twist by having a woman confess to her lover that she has had a checkered past—at the age of five:

> I was often kissed 'neath the mistletoe
> By small boys excited by tea,
> If I knew that you existed,
> I'd have scratched them and resisted,
> But I never knew about you,
> And you never knew about me.

As Lee Davis notes, "Plum added a dimension beyond cleverness. Now, there was a unique sort of felicity and balance, a drollness, a sweetness which never dipped into stickiness."[4]

The Princess shows exerted a great influence on young lyricists and composers. Richard Rodgers sat through *Very Good Eddie* (1915) six times. "It pointed the way I wanted to go."[5] Three years later, when he met lyricist Larry Hart, Hart launched into a diatribe against Tin Pan Alley lyricists who failed to use "interior rhymes, feminine rhymes, triple rhymes and false rhymes"—indeed anything but the simplest and tritest "juxtapositions of words like 'slush' and 'mush.'"[6] Only Wodehouse was exempt from Hart's scorn, and when he found that Rodgers shared his enthusiasm for the Princess shows, the twenty-three year-old lyricist and sixteen-year-old composer spent the afternoon listening to the songs of Wodehouse and Kern on Hart's Victrola, their partnership sealed. Although it wasn't until 1925 that Rodgers and Hart would find success on Broadway, Hart would tell a newspaper interviewer about his great admiration for P. G. Wodehouse, who, although few of his songs ever became popular, was a master of the art of fitting words to music.

Similarly, Ira Gershwin recorded, in a diary he began in 1916, his admiration for the Princess shows, especially *Leave It to Jane* (1917) and *Miss 1917*. After he saw these shows, he too would listen to recordings of them again and again. Many years later, he would receive a letter from P. G. Wodehouse, telling him that, of all the great lyricists who had been inspired by the Princess shows, Ira was "the best of the whole bunch."[7]

One song from *Oh, Boy!* that did become popular was "Till the Clouds Roll By," which placed among the Top Twenty songs in June, July, and August 1917. It's easy to see why Larry Hart admired Wodehouse's rhyming skills. Taking a formulaic idea about a sudden rain shower, Wodehouse uses feminine rhymes:

> *Skies are* **weep**-ing
> *While the world is* **sleep**-ing
> *Troubles* **heap**-ing

He also uses "off" or "false" rhymes:

> *Please, I beg don't* mention it,
> *I would not* mind a bit.

Most clever are his interior rhymes that fall within rather than at the end of lines:

> *What bad* luck! It's *coming down in* buckets…
> *I've a* warm coat—*waterproof—a* storm coat …
> *Later on, too, I will ward the* grippe off *with a little* nip of *brandy.*

Such witty rhymes showed that lyrics written *to* music could be every bit as clever as Gilbert's light verse that Sullivan set to music. By following the rhythm of the music, moreover, they sounded more like casual conversation than metrically regular poetry.

Till The Clouds Roll By

Words by
JEROME KERN
P. G. WODEHOUSE
and
GUY BOLTON

Music by
JEROME KERN

Till the clouds 4

150

4

REFRAIN

rain_____ comes a pit-ter, pat - ter,_____ And I'd

like_____ to be safe in bed._____ Skies are

weep - ing_____ While the world is sleep - ing_____ Trou-ble heap-ing

On our head._____ It is

Till the clouds 4

Till the clouds 4

Henry Creamer and Turner Layton

HENRY CREAMER AND TURNER LAYTON were one of the few black songwriting teams on Tin Pan Alley. Although they wrote together for only six years, from 1918 to 1924, they created more than sixty songs. Their most enduring song, "After You've Gone" (1918), has a chorus that is only twenty measures long, rather than the standard thirty-two bars. Still, it follows the usual structure of four sections (each four rather than eight bars long) in an ABAC pattern, plus a closing four-bar tag phrase. Although it is short, the chorus is "harmonically busy, shifting chords with every measure. The first four notes of the chorus melody are the same as those of 'Peg o' My Heart'"[1] (Among songwriters, it was believed that if you want to write a new hit song, start with the first few notes of an old hit song).

Within the A sections, Layton counterpoints two short phrases, the second of which is syncopated, beginning on an eighth-note rest. That syncopated lilt inspired Henry Creamer to craft an unusual torch song (possibly named for the torch Orpheus carried through the underworld in search of his lost Eurydice). Although the first phrase is mournful, the second has a kick to it:

After you've gone [♪]and left me crying
After you've gone [♪]there's no denying.

Then when the music shifts to the B section, the lyric turns the tables on the listener's expectations—it's not the singer but the departed lover who will be mourning the loss:

You'll feel blue, you'll feel sad,
[𝄽] You'll miss the dearest pal you've ever had.

"After You've Gone" was interpolated into the Broadway musical *So Long Letty*, but despite a recording by the noted singer Marion Harris, the song did not become a hit. Not until almost ten years later, when the blues singer Bessie Smith and Sophie "Last of the Red-Hot Mamas" Tucker recorded it in 1927, did "After You've Gone" become successful. Since then, recordings by Louis Armstrong, Benny Goodman, Frank Sinatra, Judy Garland, Dinah Washington, Fiona Apple, and others have made it a standard.

AFTER YOU'VE GONE

BY
CREAMER
& LAYTON

BROADWAY MUSIC CORPORATION
WILL VON TILZER PRESIDENT
145 WEST 45TH ST NEW YORK

After You've Gone

By
CREAMER & LAYTON

Now won't you list-en dear-ie while I say How could you tell me that you're going a - way?
Don't you re-mem-ber how you used to say You'd al - ways love me in the same old way?

Don't say that we must part Don't break my ach-ing heart
And now it's ver - y strange That you should ev - er change

You know I've loved you tru - ly man - y years Loved you night and day
Sometimes I think some-one has won your heart Temp - ted you a - way

How can you leave me, can't you see my tears? List - en while I say
But let me warn you tho' we're miles a - part You'll re - gret some day

CHORUS

After you've gone and left me cry-ing   After you've gone   There's no de-ny-ing,

you'll feel blue,   You'll feel sad,   You'll miss the dear-est pal you've ev-er had

There'll come a time,   now don't for-get it, There'll come a time,   when you'll re-gret it

Some day   when you grow lone-ly   Your heart will break like mine and you'll want me on-ly

After you've gone   After you've gone a-way.

After You've Gone 2

Joseph McCarthy and Harry Carroll

TIN PAN ALLEY COMPOSERS knew that one way to write a hit was to "borrow" part of a melody from an already successful song. Their borrowings sometimes included classical music, and the self-proclaimed "Tune Detective," Sigmund Spaeth, would entertain audiences by showing them how many of their favorite songs were adaptations of classical compositions, such as Buddy Kaye and Ted Mossman's "Till the End of Time" (based on Chopin's "Polonaise in A-Flat Major") and Robert Wright and George Forest's "Stranger in Paradise" (adapted from Borodin's *Prince Igor*).

Composer Harry Carroll went to Chopin's *Fantasie Impromptu in C-Sharp Minor* when he and lyricist Joseph McCarthy were inspired by a title for a song. The inspiration came from a disparaging remark by a friend, who said, "You songwriters are an unpredictable lot. You're up in the clouds one day and lower than all hell the next."

"You know why that is, don't you," Carroll shot back. "We're always chasing rainbows." "Boy," the friend said. "You've got a song title there. A sure hit."[1] Chopin's melody gave Carroll the sweeping range he needed to inspire McCarthy's lyric about soaring and sinking through life, trying but constantly failing to find happiness.

"I'm Always Chasing Rainbows" was introduced in the Broadway musical *Oh, Look!* (1917) and has been featured in several movies, such as *Ziegfeld Girl* (1941), where it was sung by Judy Garland and Charles Winninger. The song was in the Top Twenty from August of 1918 through April 1919, then, in 1946, Perry Como's recording of "I'm Always Chasing Rainbows" was on *Your Hit Parade* for twelve weeks.

I'm Always Chasing Rainbows

Lyrics by
JOSEPH McCARTHY

Music by
HARRY CARROLL

race, just a wild goose chase, And my dreams have all been de -
nied.
Why have I al ways been a
fail - ure,
What can the rea - son be? I
rall.
dim.
won-der if the world's to blame, I won-der if it could be me?
rall.
dim.

I'm Alway Chasing Rainbows 4

4

CHORUS

I'm al - ways chas - ing rain - bows,

Watch - ing clouds drift - ing by.

My schemes are just like all my dreams, End - ing

in the sky, Some fel - lows look and find the

I'm Alway Chasing Rainbows 4

Private Irving Berlin

SHORTLY BEFORE HIS THIRTIETH BIRTHDAY on May 11, 1918, Irving Berlin became a naturalized American citizen. A few weeks later, he was drafted. One newspaper headline declared, UNITED STATES TAKES BERLIN. By the time Irving Berlin became a soldier, World War I was winding down, but that only made his training at Camp Upton in Yaphank, Long Island, all the more frustrating. Marching, drilling, and doing "KP" (Kitchen Patrol) was arduous for a man accustomed to working at all hours, reveling in the nightlife of Broadway, then being chauffeured back to his bachelor apartment, where a cook prepared a sumptuous dinner for him before he battled insomnia until he fell asleep.

"There were a lot of things about army life I didn't like," he recalled, "and the thing I didn't like most of all was reveille. I hated it. I hated it so much I used to lie awake nights thinking about how much I hated it.... That's why I finally wrote a song about it."[1] "Oh! How I Hate to Get Up in the Morning" registered not only Berlin's but everybody's resistance to regimentation. Tying the melody's insistent bugle-call figure to the vernacular catchphrase "You've got to get up," Berlin found another perfect match of words to music. Skillfully building his song to its climax, he repeats the musical title phrase but instead of a helpless lament, the lyric turns aggressive:

> *Someday I'm going to murder the bugler,*
> *Someday they're going to find him dead.*
> *I'll amputate his reveille and step upon it heavily,*
> *And spend the rest of my life in bed.*

A song that begins so pathetically comes to a rousing finale as the soldier glories in his fantasy of revenge.

"Oh! How I Hate to Get Up in the Morning" became popular among soldiers as well as civilians. As opposed to the rousing jingoism of Cohan's "Over

There," Berlin's insubordinate daydream appealed to soldiers and everybody else who has to live by the clock. The success of the song helped Berlin escape reveille forever. As his songwriter friend and fellow soldier Harry Ruby recalled, Berlin was so frustrated with army routine that he devised an "angle." Learning that the Navy had staged a successful fund-raising show at the Century Theater, Berlin pitched an idea to Major General J. Franklin Bell:

> Do you know how many people are in this Army who are from show business? The camp is full of them. Fine actors, vaudeville headliners…acrobats, singers—you never saw anything like it. Why don't we put on a show with these people? We could even play it on Broadway in one of the theatres—boost morale, help recruiting, everything![2]

Whether the general was motivated by traditional rivalry with the Navy or whether he thought such a show could raise money for one of his own pet projects—a community house on the base where relatives could visit soldiers—he gave Berlin the go-ahead.

At that point, according to Ruby, Berlin worked his "angle": "But here's the thing, General," he says, "I write at night. Sometimes I work all night when I get an idea. And I couldn't do that if I had to get up in the morning at five, you understand." "Why, you don't have to get up at five," says the General. "You just forget about all that. *You write this show.*"[3]

What started as a ploy to avoid reveille launched Berlin's career as a producer. He commandeered the huge Century Theatre, summoned three hundred soldiers as his cast and crew, and started rehearsals for a revue called *Yip! Yip! Yaphank!* He wrote songs that satirized army life. Knowing that the Navy revue had featured sailors in drag, Berlin staged productions that spoofed Ziegfeld's lavish glorifications of the American girl. In a blackface number, "The Sterling Silver Moon," soldiers serenaded a beautiful black woman, the only woman in the show:

My pretty Mandy,
Don't you know the parson is handy?
Come and talk it over with Andy
'Neath the sterling silver moon.

The name "Mandy" featured so prominently in the lyric that audiences remembered it as the title, so Berlin withdrew the sheet music for "The Sterling Silver Moon" and reissued it as "Mandy." Then in 1919, when he wrote songs for the *Ziegfeld Follies,* he reworked the song musically and lyrically and created some clever internal rhymes:

Here's the ring *for your* fing*er.*
*Isn't it a hum*ding*er?*

The highlight of *Yip! Yip! Yaphank*, however, was Berlin's own rendition of "Oh! How I Hate to Get Up in the Morning" as he was dragged out of his pup tent, bleary-eyed and yawning, by two burly soldiers.

When Berlin used "Oh! How I Hate to Get Up in the Morning" in *Yip! Yip! Yaphank*, he wrote a different verse so that he could sing the song himself. Instead of reporting the lament of "a soldier friend of mine," Berlin gives voice to his own frustration:

> *I've been a soldier quite a while*
> *And I would like to state*
> *The life is simply wonderful,*
> *The army food is great.*
> *I sleep with ninety-seven others*
> *In a wooden hut;*
> *I love them all; they all love me—*
> *It's very lovely, but*

This is the verse Berlin sang in *This Is the Army*, his all-soldier show of World War II.

He also rewrote the ending of the second chorus—probably at the same time. While *Yip! Yip! Yaphank* was produced shortly before the armistice, when victory was in clear sight, *This Is the Army* played before troops in 1942, at the darkest point of the war. It was hard to imagine "the minute the battle is over" or "the minute the foe is dead," so Berlin decided to revise the lyric to:

> *Someday I'm going to murder the bugler;*
> *Someday they're going to find him dead—*
> *And then I'll get that other pup,*
> *The one that wakes the bugler up,*
> *And spend the rest of my life in bed.*

This is the version Berlin sang in the film version of *This Is the Army*—wearing his World War I uniform.

For the finale of the show, Berlin wrote a march, "We're on Our Way to France," sung by the entire company in full battle gear as they marched off the stage on ramps and up the aisles through the audience. The song connected the world of theater with the "theater" of war. That connection became even more real on the last night of the show's run. The company had just received orders to board a troop carrier bound for France. As they marched up the aisles, they continued marching out of the theater and down the street as the audience realized that the cast was literally marching off to war. Before they boarded the troop ship, however, the armistice was signed on November 11, 1918, and Irving Berlin, by now Sergeant Irving Berlin, returned to civilian life.

Dedicated to my friend "Private Howard Friend" who occupies the cot next to mine and feels as I do about the "bugler"

Oh! How I Hate To Get Up In The Morning.

By IRVING BERLIN.

The oth - er day I / A bu - gler in the

chanced to meet a sol - dier friend of mine, — He'd been in camp for sev - 'ral weeks and / arm - y is the luck - i - est of men, — He wakes the boys at five and then goes

he was look - ing fine; — His mus - cles had de - vel - oped and his cheeks were ros - y / back to bed a - gain; — He does - n't have to blow a - gain un - til the af - ter-

red, — I asked him how he liked the life, and this is what he said: / noon, — If ev - 'ry thing goes well with me I'll be a bu - gler soon.

801

F.J.LAWSON CO.N.Y.

The *Ziegfeld Follies*

◆◆◆

FLORENZ ZIEGFELD WAS BORN in Chicago to a German father and a Belgian mother. Although his father was Lutheran and his mother Roman Catholic, "Flo" Ziegfeld himself was not religious and, in later life, dreaded the finality of death. As a child, he evinced a flair for showmanship, selling tickets to neighborhood kids to watch a bowl of water in which, he told them, there were invisible fish. In 1893, he opened a nightclub to attract the crowds who came to the Chicago World's Fair. When audiences did not flock to The Trocadero, however, he brought in a strong man, Eugene Sandow, and built up publicity for the feats of strength he would perform. Sandow's performance—and his fifty-eight-inch chest—attracted massive crowds that included numerous society matrons.

Ziegfeld's success with Sandow spurred him to try his entrepreneurial skills on Broadway. After persuading the comedy team of Charles Evans and Bill Hoey to let him mount a musical version of their comic play *A Parlor Match*, Ziegfeld sailed for Europe in search of a leading lady. He was intrigued by Anna Held, the darling of Parisian café society, with her eighteen-inch waist and saucy stage persona. Even though she was under contract with the *Folies Bergère*, Ziegfeld wooed her not only commercially but, as he would do with so many of his beautiful performers, romantically as well. When Held agreed to become his star as well as his mistress, Ziegfeld asked his friend "Diamond Jim" Brady to wire $1,500 to the *Folies Bergère* to buy out her contract.

Held's rendition of "Won't You Come and Play with Me?" in the 1896 production of *A Parlor Match* lived up to all the publicity Ziegfeld had generated for her. He even told the press she took milk baths (which in actuality was just water that turned milky when perfumed). From 1896 through 1908, Ziegfeld staged musical shows designed to showcase Held's charms, even adding a chorus line, "The Anna Held Girls," to back her numbers.

In 1907, Anna Held suggested that Ziegfeld produce an American version of the *Folies Bergère*, injecting a dose of Parisian sexiness into the American revue format of comic sketches and songs. After a successful New York run and an equally successful tour, the first edition of his *Follies* brought in more than $130,000 on an investment of only $13,800. The revues provided a showcase for Tin Pan Alley songs, such as "Shine On, Harvest Moon" (1908) and "By the Light of the Silvery Moon" (1909), both sung by Nora Bayes, who, Ziegfeld told reporters, ate nothing but lollipops.

Beginning in 1911, Ziegfeld continued producing his annual *Follies*, which he called the *Ziegfeld Follies*. He brought in such talented comics as Fanny Brice, Eddie Cantor, W. C. Fields, Ed Wynn, Will Rogers, and, in a daring gesture, Bert Williams, the first black performer to appear on Broadway alongside whites. Ziegfeld's annual shows featured sets and costumes that were lavish yet tasteful compared to the shabby revues of the penny-pinching Shubert brothers. His designer, Joseph Urban, "rid musicals of tasteless, kaleidoscope of colors that had splashed across every scene.... Urban carefully controlled his colors, not only limiting them to shades of a single color within a scene, but frequently seeing to it that they flowed gently from one scene into the next."[1]

In his sets, Urban used huge staircases to display Ziegfeld's girls as well as a glass walkway so they could dance above the customers' heads. Ziegfeld's revues were distinctly different from other Broadway shows that were "a hodgepodge of crosstalk, slapstick, songs, and burlesque. Ziegfeld's innovation was to see the revue not as a melee, but as an elegant environment in which to display the hitherto most anonymous person in the musical theatre—the chorus girl."[2]

Ziegfeld lavished money on sets and costumes that featured these girls who seldom sang or danced—merely walked or stood or sat. The investment paid off as audiences were willing to pay as much as $5.00 for tickets to enjoy the sumptuous spectacles. Although Ziegfeld usually used songs by a variety of songwriters, he asked Irving Berlin to write most of the songs for the *Follies of 1919*. Ziegfeld had been impressed by *Yip! Yip! Yaphank* and used one of its numbers, "Mandy," to feature Marilyn Miller. Bert Williams sang Berlin's rhythmic dance number "You Cannot Make Your Shimmy Shake on Tea," one of several songs, including "Prohibition" and "A Syncopated Cocktail," that poked fun at the Volstead Act's ban on the sale and consumption of alcoholic beverages. Eddie Cantor had a big hit with "You'd Be Surprised," rolling his "banjo eyes" suggestively over the surprising prowess of an unassuming lover:

He's not so good in a crowd,
But when you get him alone,
You'd be surprised.

Also pleasantly surprising for both Berlin and Ziegfeld were the sales for Cantor's recording of "You'd Be Surprised." While recordings had been made since the early days of Tin Pan Alley, they were still regarded by music publishers as a sideline to sheet-music sales. But as their technical quality improved and more homes purchased Victrolas, records began to rival sheet music as the mainstay of the music business. Cantor's recording of "You'd Be Surprised" sold 800,000 copies—equaling its sheet-music sales.

Berlin's greatest triumph in the *Ziegfeld Follies of 1919* was "A Pretty Girl Is Like a Melody," a paean to the American ideal of femininity. Comparing its musical quality to a song like "Mandy," Alec Wilder concludes, "it is extraordinary that such a development in style and sophistication should have taken place in a single year."[3] Its sweeping melody that drives forward in subtly surprising contours is as beautiful as anything the classically trained Jerome Kern had written. The lyric is equally graceful—and forceful, elaborating a single extended simile in colloquial terms: a pretty girl is like an insistent melody that at first "haunts" your mind, then starts a ghostly "marathon" that gives your mind the "run-around," then finally produces a "strain"—at once musical and muscular—as her fleeting image reverses itself and imprisons her pursuer. In the end, "you can't escape" because, paradoxically, "she's in your memory":

> *She will leave you and then*
> *Come back again.*

By breaking up this lyrical phrase against his chromatic melody, Berlin portrays not so much a flesh-and-blood woman but a tantalizing ideal of seductive beauty, the perfect evocation of Ziegfeld's gossamer illusions.

Ironically, "A Pretty Girl Is Like a Melody" was added to the *Ziegfeld Follies of 1919* as an afterthought. Berlin had completed the rest of the score when Ziegfeld beseeched him for one more song. Showing Berlin color plates of expensive costumes he had ordered for his lovelies, the impresario said, "Look at these costumes. I have to have a number for them; my bookkeeper will kill me." "So I went home," Berlin said, "I looked at the costume plates. I thought of melodies to go with each girl and gown. 'Traumerei,' Viennese waltz, etc. But I had to have a song to introduce the number and close it. Then I wrote lyrics and music to fit the action."[4] "A Pretty Girl Is Like a Melody" was the number one song in October 1919 and stayed in the Top Ten for three months. Years later, Berlin reflected on how the song had endured as a standard: "Today they play it when a pretty girl walks across the stage...and strip-teasers disrobe to it. That's show business."[5]

A Pretty Girl Is Like A Melody

Words and Music by
IRVING BERLIN

A Pretty Girl 4

4

A Pretty Girl 4

George Gershwin

LIKE MOST SONGWRITING TEAMS, George and Ira Gershwin were polar opposites. George was dynamic, aggressive, always the center of attention. As a boy, he excelled in roller-skating and street-fighting; he bragged to a friend that he'd had his first girl at the age of nine. Ira was shy, withdrawn, bookish; George often referred to him as "My brother Ira, the scholar." Because Ira did so well at school, he was frequently the family representative who had to meet with the principal about his younger brother's bad behavior.

But George changed one day in 1910 when a second-hand piano was delivered to his family's apartment on Second Avenue in Manhattan. The piano was intended for Ira, but George rushed over to it and, miraculously it seemed to Rose and Morris Gershvin (the family name, changed from the original "Gershovitz"), began to play. George didn't tell his parents that he had taught himself to play on a friend's piano. The trick worked. George got piano lessons, and Ira got to go back to his books.

George studied classical music, but what he really wanted to do was write popular songs; at the age of fifteen he quit high school and went to work at the Remick Music Company as a "plugger"—the youngest plugger on Tin Pan Alley. After playing piano all day, Gershwin frequently spent his evenings in Harlem, where he emulated the wide-ranging "stride piano" style of jazz musicians such as Willie "The Lion" Smith and Luckey Roberts.

When he tried writing his own songs for Remick's, however, he was told by his boss, "You're here to *play* songs, Gershwin—not write them."

But write songs he did.

In 1916, his first composition was given a long title by his lyricist, Murray Roth: "When You Want 'Em You Can't Get 'Em, When You Got 'Em You Don't Want 'Em." For the next three years, George kept cranking out melodies for Tin

Pan Alley firms. But from the very beginning he was looking beyond Tin Pan Alley to Broadway, convinced that songs written for musical theater could bring sophistication to the simple formulas of popular song. Several of his songs were interpolated into Broadway shows, and he landed a job as staff composer at T. B. Harms, a music publishing firm that specialized in songs for musical theater. With the blessing of Max Dreyfus, who had taken over Harms, George could moonlight as a rehearsal pianist for Broadway shows. One of the shows he worked for had a score by Jerome Kern, and the older composer took George under his wing.

Despite Kern's encouragement, no opportunity emerged for George to write a score for a Broadway musical, so George tried a different strategy. One day Irving Berlin showed up at Harms with a new song, "That Revolutionary Rag," inspired by the Russian Revolution. When he demonstrated it, Dreyfus took "That Revolutionary Rag" on the spot. It was an open secret, however, that Berlin could not read music.

"I need someone to write it down for me," he told Dreyfus.

Dreyfus summoned George, who dutifully took the song down in musical notation, then performed his own arrangement of it.

"It was so good," Berlin later said, "I hardly recognized it."[1]

Knowing that Berlin had recently left the sheet-music publishing firm of Waterson, Berlin, and Snyder to establish his own firm, Gershwin thought he might need a new "musical secretary" to notate and arrange his songs. When he asked for the job, Berlin told Gershwin to play some of his own songs. As he did, Berlin realized that Gershwin was too talented to merely notate the songs of another composer. "Stick to writing your own songs, kid," Berlin told him.[2]

Shortly afterwards, George finally got the opportunity he'd been yearning for. Alex Aarons, the son of a successful Broadway producer, had been given the chance by his father to produce his first musical show, *La-La-Lucille!* Aarons was looking for a composer to work with his lyricists, Arthur Jackson and Buddy DeSylva. "Every career needs a lucky break to start it on its way," Gershwin later said, "and my lucky break came in 1919 when I was brought to Alex Aarons...I was twenty years old at the time, and Arthur Jackson, the lyric writer, was the man who brought us together. After hearing a few of my tunes, Alex Aarons decided to engage me as composer for his first show, *La-La-Lucille!* This was very brave of him, because I was quite inexperienced at the time, never having written a complete score."[3] Although Gershwin's music got little recognition, *La-La-Lucille!* did well during the summer of 1919 until it was closed by the Actors' Equity Strike in August.

Then lightning struck again—but it took a while.

Back in 1918, George was having dinner at Dinty Moore's restaurant on Times Square with lyricist Irving Caesar. Caesar suggested they try to cash in on the popularity of the song "Hindustan," by writing their own knockoff of the sprightly "one step" in $\frac{2}{4}$ time. "Why don't we write an American one-step, George?"[4]

Gershwin was intrigued by the idea, and, as they took the Fifth Avenue bus up to the Gershwin family apartment on 144th Street, he got some ideas for the melody, and Caesar had blocked out a lyric. Caesar also suggested the title should be based on Stephen Foster's "Old Folks at Home," with its opening line, "Way down upon the Swanee River."

Once at the Gershwin apartment, they finished the song while George's father was playing poker with his cronies in the next room. As Caesar recalled:

> In about fifteen minutes we had turned out "Swanee," verse and chorus. But we thought the song should have a trio and for a few minutes were deciding about this addition. The losers in the game kept saying, "Boys, finish it some other time," and the lucky ones urged us to complete the song right there and then. This we did, and old Gershwin lost not a moment in fetching a comb, over which he superimposed some tissue while George and I sang it over and over again at the insistence of the winning poker players.[5]

While basically a Tin Pan Alley song, Gershwin's music had some sophisticated touches—rhythmic momentum and a change of key between verse and chorus—and Caesar's lyrics had flashes of vernacular humor, such as accenting "**How** I love you" (instead of "How I **love** you") and spelling out "D-I-X-I-E that's where my Mammy's waitin' for me."

At the time, George was working as a rehearsal pianist for a revue at the New Amsterdam Theatre, so he and Caesar demonstrated "Swanee" for the director, Ned Wayburn. Wayburn liked the song and agreed to use it in a revue he would be staging at the Capitol Theatre once the theater was completed. Although the songwriters would have to wait a year before "Swanee" was introduced, they agreed because the Capitol would be the largest movie theater in America. Like many such theaters, it would also feature vaudeville shows that offered a sound component to complement silent films, along with preserving live stage entertainment. Once the Capitol was completed in October 1919, Wayburn featured "Swanee" in a huge production number with fifty dancers who had tiny electric lights on the tips of their shoes.

Despite that spectacular debut, "Swanee" went nowhere.

Later in the year, George Gershwin was invited to a party where Al Jolson was present. As usual, George wound up at the piano, dynamically performing his own songs. When Jolson heard "Swanee," he offered to add it as an interpolation to his touring show *Sinbad*. Jolson recorded the song in January 1920, and it became a huge hit. Max Dreyfus ran an ad on the front page of *Variety* saying "Swanee" was "Al Jolson's Greatest Song," and sheet-music and record sales soon hit the millions. It was in the Top Ten from March through July 1920.

Ironically, it was this Tin Pan Alley song that finally catapulted George Gershwin to Broadway. There, as Gerald Bordman notes, he would bring the "far more angular melodic lines" of jazz to his songs rather than the "curvilinear lines of operetta…classical harmonies were interspersed with fresh, narrow, 'bluesy' modulations, while the more gently flowing tempos of the older schools were replaced by the more staccato, excited tempos, as well as by the distinctive languor of pure blues. The resulting sound was steely, often sardonic, and always thoroughly contemporary."[6] Even though most of these later songs would be written for Broadway musicals, "Swanee," a Tin Pan Alley song, remains the biggest selling song of George Gershwin's career.

Swanee

Words by
I. CAESAR

Music by
GEORGE GERSHWIN

Allegro moderato

Piano

I've been a - way from you a long time ___ I nev-er

thought I'd miss you so ___ Some-how I feel

Your love was real Near you I long to be ___

5935-4 Swanee

5935_4 Swanee

5935 - 4 Swanee

Otto Harbach

OTTO HARBACH WAS OLDER than most of his songwriting contemporaries. He was born in 1873 to Danish immigrants whose surname was Christiansen. Shortly after settling in Salt Lake City in the 1830s, his parents changed their name to Hauerbach, the name of their employer's farm, "a common practice at the time," according to Thomas Hischak.[1] Otto kept the name Hauerbach until World War I, when he changed it to Harbach in the face of anti-German sentiment.

He went to Knox College in Illinois, taught at Whitman College in Washington State, then moved to New York City to pursue a doctorate in English at Columbia University. In 1902, as he was riding a streetcar, he saw a billboard for a Broadway musical that had a picture of Fay Templeton Harbach was so enthralled by her beauty that he gave up graduate school and went into show business.

At a time when songs in musicals bore little relation to character and dramatic situation, Otto Harbach's literary background prompted him to write musical plays and lyrics that integrated story, characters, and songs. Over the course of his career, he wrote the book and lyrics for more than forty musicals, and at one point in 1925, he had five hit musicals running on Broadway simultaneously—something no one has done before or since. Harbach also mentored younger lyricists, such as Oscar Hammerstein, on how to write books and songs where lyrics fit integrally with the characters and story. As a result of Harbach's tutelage, Oscar Hammerstein went on to write the book and lyrics for such "integrated" musicals such as *Show Boat* and *Oklahoma!*

In 1920, Harbach had his first big hit song with composer Louis Hirsch in the musical *Mary.* That musical was one of several shows that were dubbed "Cinderella" musicals because the story centered on a working-class heroine, frequently Irish, who marries her boss's son or by some similar turn of plot moves up the social ladder. By Martin Bordman's count, of the hundred and twenty musicals produced between 1921 and 1924 "half were either operettas or revues. Of the fifty-eight that could be branded musical comedy, no fewer than twenty-one centered on a Cinderella figure. In short, over a sixth of all musicals and well over a third of all musical comedies employed the same basic story."[2]

Three of the earliest of these Cinderella musicals each produced a hit song: *Irene* (1919) had "Alice Blue Gown"; *Mary* (1920) featured "The Love Nest"; and *Sally* (1921) had as its big number "Look for the Silver Lining." *Mary* was so popular in its out-of-town tryouts that "The Love Nest" was already a hit when the show reached New York. It broke into the Top Ten in August 1920 and stayed there through December, with two months, September and October, as the number one song in the country. Harbach's lyric takes a title phrase usually associated with a "den of iniquity," where a philanderer maintains his mistress, and turns it into a picture of domestic bliss. George Burns and Gracie Allen used "The Love Nest" as their theme song on radio and television for many years.

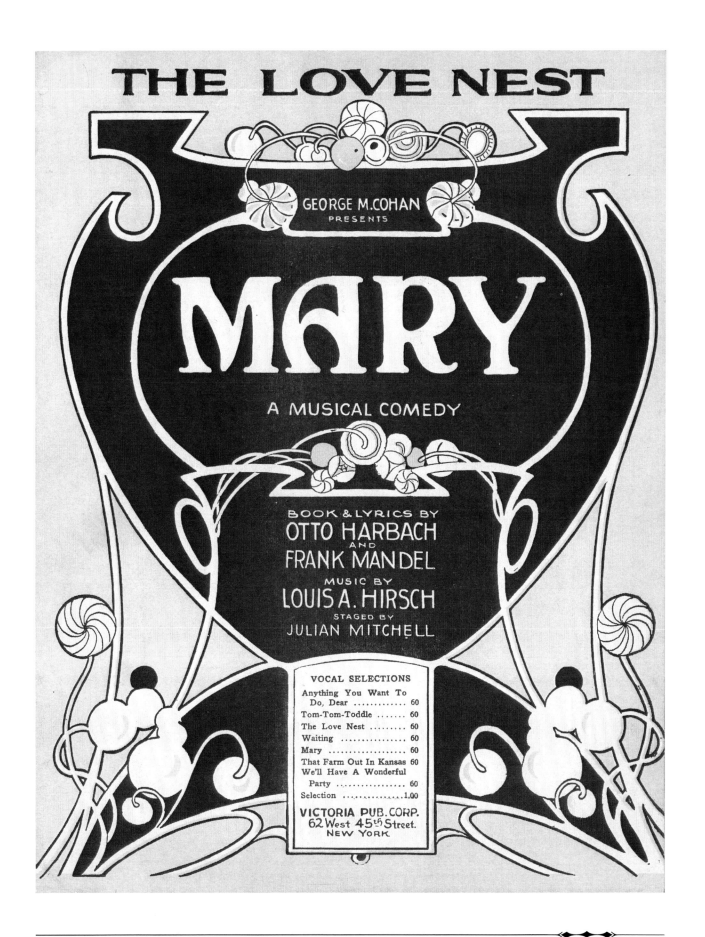

The Love Nest
(Jack and Mary)

Words by
OTTO HARBACH

Music by
LOUIS A. HIRSCH

114-4 The Love Nest

4

Like a dove rest——— Down on a farm———

A ver - an - da with some sort of cling - ing vine———

Then a kitch - en where some ramb - ler ros - es twine———

Then a small room——— Tea set of blue———

5

114-4 The Love Nest

Buddy DeSylva

ALOYSIUS DESYLVA was a Portuguese vaudeville performer whose stage name was Hal de Forest, the English equivalent of "Aloysius DeSylva." While he was performing in Azusa, California, Aloysius met the love of his life, a girl named Georgetta Gard. But her father, the sheriff of Azusa, insisted his prospective son-in-law quit show business and go into a respectable profession. Although he complied by going to law school and opening a legal practice, Aloysius was determined that his son, George Gard DeSylva, would be a star in show business. By the age of four, little George, whose nickname was "Buddy," made his debut in a song-and-dance act on the vaudeville circuit.

Grandfather Gard still called the shots though; he insisted that Buddy get an education. He graduated from Citrus Union High School in Azusa and went on to the University of Southern California. There he formed a singing group, the Hawaiians, with three classmates who accompanied themselves on ukuleles. Buddy DeSylva wrote songs for the group, and one of the people who heard the Hawaiians perform was Al Jolson. Jolson agreed to record some of their songs, but, as usual, he insisted on a "cut-in"—that his name appear on the sheet music and records as one of the composers so that he got a share of the song's royalties. In 1919, when Buddy DeSylva was a sophomore, he received a royalty check for $16,000. He promptly quit college and moved to New York.

He was hired as a staff lyricist at Remick's, and one of his first songs, "Avalon," which he wrote in 1921 with composer Vincent Rose, was a hit. "Avalon" was America's number one song in January of 1921. But no sooner did "Avalon" become a hit than the songwriters were sued by Giacomo Puccini, who charged that they had taken the melody from "El lucevan le stele," one of his arias in *Tosca*. Puccini won the lawsuit and received $25,000 plus royalties from sales of sheet music and recordings.

While the melody may have been plagiarized, Buddy DeSylva's lyric was original and authentic. Unlike many Tin Pan Alley songwriters who wrote songs about Alabama and Carolina even though they had never been south of Philadelphia, Buddy DeSylva had grown up in southern California where Avalon was a resort town on Santa Catalina Island. In Avalon, Buddy knew, "tuna clippers" sailed in the bay. With "Avalon" and other songs for Al Jolson such as "California Here I Come," Buddy DeSylva celebrated his home state as a "land of dreams."[1]

AVALON
FOX TROT SONG

Lyric and Music by
AL JOLSON
and VINCENT ROSE

Arr. by J. BODEWALT LAMPE

Ev – 'ry   morn-ing mem-'ries stray   A- cross the
Just be – fore I sail'd a – way   She said the

2122-4

Avalon - 4

198

4

CHORUS *semplice*

I found my love in A - va - lon _____ Be -

- side _____ the bay _____ I

left my love in A - va - lon _____ and

sail'd _____ a - way _____ I

Avalon – 4

Avalon—4

Buddy DeSylva's success on Tin Pan Alley with such songs as "Avalon" garnered him the chance to work on Broadway—and with no less a composer than Jerome Kern. With Kern, DeSylva wrote the score for *Sally* in 1921, another of the "Cinderella" musicals. *Sally* was closer to the Cinderella motif than other shows because its main character, played by Marilyn Miller in her first leading role on Broadway, is an orphan who washes dishes in an inn. Its big hit, "Look for the Silver Lining," was what was called a "Pollyanna" song. Named after the irrepressibly optimistic heroine of Eleanor Porter's 1913 novel, "Pollyanna" songs were meant to cheer up the hero or heroine of a musical just when everything looked dark and gloomy.

Sally was produced by Florenz Ziegfeld (who was having an affair with Miller) and ran for a staggering 520 performances. DeSylva's lyric for "Look for the Silver Lining" included such optimistic platitudes as

A heart full of joy and gladness
Will always banish sadness and strife
So always look for the silver lining

While such upbeat lyrics might suit Marilyn Miller in her Cinderella role as "Sally," they were a far cry from her fiery behavior backstage. One night during the run of *Sally*, Ziegfeld brought his daughter to Marilyn Miller's dressing room after the performance.

Ignoring the child, Miller greeted Ziegfeld by saying, "Hello, you lousy son of a bitch!"

Ziegfeld pushed his daughter toward Miller in an effort to stem her tirade. "You've heard me talk about Patricia," he stammered.

"Yes," Miller shot back, "to the point of nausea!"

She then threw one of her costumes at Ziegfeld and shouted, "This piece of crap you call a costume—you can take it and shove it!"[2]

To placate Miller, Ziegfeld provided her with new costumes every night and had her dressing room redecorated in satin and velvet. Miller had found the silver lining indeed.

Still, nothing could brighten the troubled waters of the show. After its spectacularly successful three-year run, Jerome Kern confided to a friend that *Sally* was the only one of his hit shows he actually hated. His bitterness may reflect his own frustration with Miller's mercurial temper but also his dissatisfaction with the superficial nature of early 1920s musicals, particular those of the Cinderella variety. The sophisticated Princess shows were behind him, but ahead was the magnificent musical drama of *Show Boat* (1927). Still, "Look for the Silver Lining" remains one of Kern's most enduring songs, As Gerald Bordman observed, it "is simple harmonically, with few jumps and written mostly in quarter, half, and whole notes. Two features stand out. One is the fifteenth and sixteenth measures, where a series of dotted quarter and eighth notes, sung over the words 'do is make it shine for you,' leads fetchingly back to the main theme. . . . The other feature is less obvious. It is the small jump . . . from *b* flat to *e* flat . . . in the sixth bar over the second syllable of 'appears.' Until this point the song has moved with amazing tightness, only once skipping more than a full tone."[3] "Look for the Silver Lining" was sung movingly by Judy Garland in *Till the Clouds Roll By* (1946), Kern's film biography.

2

Look For The Silver Lining

Duet

(Blair and Sally)

Words by
BUD DE SYLVA

Music by
JEROME KERN

(Blair) Please don't be of-fend-ed if I preach to you a while,
(Sally) As I wash my dish-es, I'll be fol-low-ing your plan,

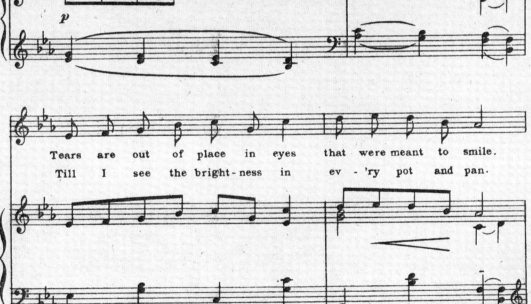

Tears are out of place in eyes that were meant to smile.
Till I see the bright-ness in ev-'ry pot and pan.

T. B. H. Co. 171-4

There's a way to make your ver - y big-gest troub-les small,
I am sure your point of view will ease the dai - ly grind,

Here's the hap-py se-cret of it all. _____
So I'll keep re-peat-ing in my mind. _____

Burthen

p–f

Look for _____ the sil - ver lin - ing _____

_____ When - e'er a cloud ap - pears in the

4

blue_____ Re - mem - ber some - where_____ the sun is shin - ing_____ And so the right thing _____ to do is make it shine for you. A heart full _____ of joy and

Noble Sissle and
Eubie Blake

WHILE THE BROADWAY MUSICAL stage was largely off-limits to African Americans in the early twentieth century, vaudeville sometimes allowed a black act on the bill—but never more than one. That's the reason why the musical team of James Hubert (Eubie) Blake and Noble Sissle had not met the comedy duo of Flournay E. Miller and Aubrey Lyles until the two acts performed at a National Association for the Advancement of Colored People (NAACP) benefit in 1920. Talking backstage, the four men decided to put on an all-black musical.

Shuffle Along was little more than an expansion of their vaudeville acts around a story about a mayoral election in which all the candidates but one, whose name is Harry, are corrupt. They booked it in a lecture hall, far from Broadway, that didn't have an orchestra pit or a full stage. They salvaged sets and costumes from two recent Broadway flops, and even though the costumes had sweat stains under the arms, they could not afford to have them cleaned.

The big hit of the show, "I'm Just Wild About Harry," was originally written by Eubie Blake as a romantic Viennese waltz. But Lottie Gee, the singer who introduced it, asked "How can you have a waltz in a colored show? Make it a one-step."

"That cut me to the quick," Blake said. "She was going to destroy my beautiful melody. I loved that waltz. Then Sissle went along with her…'All right,' I said, 'We'll make it a one-step.'"[1]

"I'm Just Wild About Harry" did not go over well with out-of-town audiences, and Sissle and Blake nearly dropped it from *Shuffle Along*. But just before the show opened in New York, they replaced a sick chorus boy with a member of the singing ensemble. During Gee's rendition of "I'm Just Wild About Harry," the new chorus member could not follow the dance routine, so, as Sissle explained, "he dropped out of the line and with a jive smile and a high-stepping routine of his own, he stopped the show cold."[2] The song—and dance—helped make *Shuffle Along* a hit; the show ran fourteen months on Broadway. The song itself remained in the Top Ten from July through September 1922. As Robert Kimball and William Bolcom note, *Shuffle Along* "was one of the few Broadway shows of the decade to run more than five hundred performances."[3]

While "I'm Just Wild About Harry" was the hit of the show, the ballad "Love Will Find a Way" broke the taboo against romantic duets between blacks. White audiences, it was feared, would find serious romantic expression in song ludicrous if it were sung by black characters. In coon songs such as '"Hello, Ma Baby," love was always portrayed comically. "Honest, unburlesqued romantic love interest in a black show was dangerous ground," observe Kimball and Bolcom. "White audiences might be expected to boo the show off the stage."[4] "On opening night in New York," Sissle recalled, "this song had us more worried than anything else in the show. We were afraid that when Lottie Gee and Roger Matthews sang it, we'd be run out of town. . . . Imagine our amazement when the song was not only beautifully received but encored."[5]

The success of *Shuffle Along*, according to David Jasen and Gene Jones, was largely based on Eubie Blake's music:

> Blake alone among black writers of the 1920s thought of himself as a theatre composer. Others wrote songs for shows; he wrote scores. He had loved theatre music since he was a teenager, and he had great respect for the writing of it. His love songs have a theatrical passion and range not found in those of Fats Waller or James P. Johnson. Their ballads flirt, but Blake's are declarative, and musically bigger than anyone else's. Syncopation is the pulse of his show music, but melody is its heart.[6]

Shuffle Along sparked a new interest in African American music, art, and literature that led to the "Harlem Renaissance" of the 1920s.

3

I'm Just Wild About Harry

Fox Trot Song

Words and Music by
NOBLE SISSLE and
EUBIE BLAKE

There's just one fel - low for me in this world___ Har-ry's his name___

There are some fel - lows that like all the girls,___ I mean the vamps,___

That's what I claim___ Why for ev-'ry fel - low there

With cru - el lamps,___ But my Har-ry says___ I'm the

7773

M.W.& SONS 16482-3

Copyright MCMXXI by M Witmark & Sons
International Copyright Secured

4

must be a girl___   I've found my mate___   By kind-ness of fate.___
girl of all girls,___   I'm his i-deal,___   How hap-py I feel.___

REFRAIN

I'm just wild___ a-bout Har - ry_____ and Har-ry's wild___ a-bout

me._____ The heav'n-ly bliss - es of his kiss - es

fill me with ec - sta - cy_____ He's sweet just like___ choc'-late

M.W.& SONS 16482-3

If You Are Interested In **QUARTET MUSIC** *(Sacred or Secular)* Arranged
For MALE, FEMALE and MIXED VOICES, Send For Our **CATALOG No.1**.
ENCLOSE – TWO CENT STAMP FOR POSTAGE

can - dy, and just like hon - ey from the bee

Oh, I'm just wild _ a - bout Har - ry And

he's just wild _ a - bout, can-not do _ with-out, He's just wild _ a - bout

me. me.

M.W.& SONS 16482-3

If You Are Interested In **AMATEUR MINSTRELSY** or other **ENTERTAINMENTS**
Send For Our **CATALOG No. 2** It's Full Of Good Things And Loads Of Suggestions.
ENCLOSE – TWO CENT STAMP FOR POSTAGE

212

Irving Berlin and The Music Box Theater

IRVING BERLIN'S CAREER as a businessman is almost as fascinating as his life as a songwriter. "Talent and business are wedded in him," quipped lyricist Howard Dietz, "like his words and music."[1] While Berlin started out as a lyricist who received only a few cents from sheet-music sales of his songs, he quickly realized that the real money to be made in songwriting was in publishing. He became a partner in the firm of Waterson, Berlin & Snyder, then in 1914 founded his own firm, Irving Berlin, Inc. As his own publisher, Berlin was one of the few songwriters who owned the copyrights to his songs. His experience producing *Yip! Yip! Yaphank* in 1918 also taught him that being a producer brought in more profits than writing the songs for a show. All that was needed for him to take the next step in his career was a momentous opportunity and the wisdom to take advantage of it.

The moment came in 1920 in the person of Sam Harris. Like Berlin, Harris had come up through the Lower East Side, climbing his way from working in a laundry to owning one, then branching out into boxing promotion and theatrical production. Harris had been George M. Cohan's partner ever since he helped Cohan produce his first successful musical, *Little Johnny Jones*, in 1904. Their partnership soured, however, when Cohan refused to accept the compromise that settled the Actors Equity strike of 1919, paying actors for time spent in rehearsals and no longer requiring them to supply their own costumes. Cohan's obstinacy ostracized him from the theatrical community, and Harris went looking for another partner.

Harris remembered a tip Irving Berlin had given him at a Friars' gathering: "If you ever want to build a theater just for musical comedy," the songwriter suggested, "why not call it the Music Box?" In the spring of 1920, Harris purchased a row of brownstone apartments near Broadway and 45th Street in the heart of the theater district. Hoping to engage Berlin as his new partner, Harris got on the phone and said, "I called you up to tell you that you can have your Music Box whenever you want it."[2]

Building a theater was an expensive and risky undertaking in the early 1920s. The American economy was still recovering from its postwar slump, and no one could foresee the boom years that lay ahead. The Music Box, moreover, would be a technological and aesthetic masterpiece, from its limestone façade, which featured a Renaissance loggia and columns, to its streamlined auditorium that had touches of the new Art Deco style, which emphasized machine-like designs, textures, and colors. Berlin brought the same demanding artistry to building a theater that he did to crafting a song. As expenses mounted and details of the construction spread through the Broadway community, the Music Box looked like it would be Berlin's first folly. "The boys think they're building a monument," quipped one performer about Berlin and Harris, "but they're building a tombstone."[3]

When Harris and Berlin's funds were depleted, Berlin turned to one of his oldest friends. Joe Schenck had been a clerk at Olliffe's Drugstore in Chinatown and had known Berlin when he was a singing waiter at the nearby Pelham Café. When Izzy's tips fell off, Joe Schenck would help him with his rent. Just as Izzy had gone into Tin Pan Alley, Joe Schenck had abandoned the pharmacy and gotten in on the ground floor of another new American entertainment enterprise—the film industry. Still largely based in New York rather than Hollywood, movies had started out as storefront "nickelodeons" aimed at an audience of lower-class, immigrant workers. The fact that these early films were silent and depended on mime acting made them easy to follow for audiences who spoke little English. But by 1920, in the hands of directors such as D. W. Griffith and stars such as Charlie Chaplin, films were reaching a huge and broad-based audience, and Joe Schenck became a major film producer.

He listened sympathetically to his old friend's plea for help, though at first he misconstrued it.

"I'm in trouble," Berlin stammered.

"Okay," Schenck shot back. "Who is she?"

"It's not a girl," Berlin explained. "It's a theater."

After hearing his friend out, Schenck said, "Done. Here's a check." Still, he felt he had to add a caution: "Irving, all I've put in this is some money; you've put your heart."[4]

In return for putting up the needed funds, Schenck wanted a partnership in the Music Box, but his business acumen must have warned him it was a risky investment. Just building the theater would cost nearly a million dollars—an astronomical figure for 1920—and mounting the first production would cost nearly

$200,000, more than three times the expense for the most lavish revue. Revues, moreover, were becoming increasingly commonplace on Broadway. Berlin's *Music Box Revue* would have to compete not only against Ziegfeld's annual *Follies* but against its many imitators, such as George White's *Scandals*, Edgar Selwyn's *Snapshots*, and other loose assemblages of songs, comic skits, and dances.

New York audiences had already begun to tire of the formulaic glamor of these shows, so producers relied on profits from extensive tours in other cities. But Berlin and Harris lacked the road companies for such tours. On top of that, other revue producers followed Ziegfeld's practice of using interpolated songs by a variety of composers, but Irving Berlin's fierce sense of independence would brook no interpolations. He and he alone would write all the songs for Music Box revues. "The Music Box," as Laurence Bergreen observed, "would be the first and only Broadway theater ever built to accommodate the songs and scores of a single composer."[5]

Joe Schenck had indeed bet on a long shot.

As if all of these expenses weren't bad enough, Berlin chose Hassard Short as his director. Short was a notorious spendthrift who relished spectacular scenery, costumes, and special effects. To outdo Ziegfeld's standard staircase that displayed beautiful girls, Short devised a moving staircase built under the stage that would rise from the floor and lift the girls to the ceiling. When Schenck wandered into a rehearsal to check on his investment, the staircase got stuck. Instead of panicking, Schenck clapped Berlin on the back and said, "Never mind. It's no more than you or I would lose in a good stud game and never think of it again."[6]

But Berlin was determined to use his songwriting talent to avert financial disaster. "I suppose we all work best under pressure," he once said. "I can't get to work until my partners tell me that sales are falling, that the rent is increasing, that salaries are going up—all because I'm not on the job. Then I sweat blood. Absolutely, I sweat blood between 3 and 6 many mornings and when the drops that fall off my forehead hit the paper, they're notes."[7]

He wanted to write a song that would dedicate his new theater and set the standard for the revues he planned for the Music Box. Creating a spare, fifty-two note melody, he enlivened it with syncopation. It starts off with a sweeping cello-like strain with lush whole notes that the lyric matches with long *a* and *u* vowels:

> Say *it with* mu-*sic* [𝄽]
> Beau-*tiful m*u-*sic* [𝄽]

The rest at the end of each phrase abruptly cuts off the soaring melody, and, in the second section of the chorus, a rest makes the shift from long to short notes and vowels even more abrupt:

> Some-how they'd rather be kissed [𝄽]
> To the strains of Chopin or Liszt.

Berlin's masterful manipulation of vowels and consonants, notes and rests, creates a song at once traditional and modern. Equally deft are the subtle rhymes he weaves into such phrases as "A m*el*ody m*ell*ow played on the *cell*o h*el*ps Mister Cupid *al*ong."

By bringing syncopation into a ballad, Berlin paved the way for younger songwriters, such as George Gershwin, who would begin such tender ballads as "The Man I Love" and "Embraceable You" on the upbeat after a rest. Even Berlin's allusions to Chopin and Liszt (who, after all, incorporated folk rhythms into their compositions) were part of his effort to bring jazz into popular music. As he told a *Times* reporter:

> It was no more than being able to recognize what rhythm meant, and being with the times. It was the age of the automobile. The speed and snap of American jazz music is influenced by the automobile's popularity. Wagner, Beethoven, Mendelssohn, Liszt. All the masters of music knew the value of movement.... The automobile, however, is a new method of movement. All the old rhythm is gone and in its place is heard the hum of an engine, the whirr of wheels, the explosion of an exhaust. The leisurely songs that men hummed to the clatter of horse's hooves do not fit into this new rhythm. The new age demands new music for new action.[8]

Despite the doomsayers' predictions, the *Music Box Revue of 1921* delighted audiences and critics every bit as much as did Berlin's new theater. Even at the then exorbitant price of $4 a seat, the show was sold out for months and realized a profit of $400,000, providing ample returns on Berlin's, Sam Harris's, and Joe Schenck's investments. The *Times* critic Alexander Woollcott wrote of the *Music Box Revue of 1921*:

> Its bewildering contents confirmed the dark suspicion that Sam H. Harris and Irving Berlin have gone quite mad...they have built them a playhouse in West Forty-fifth Street that is a thing of beauty in itself, and then crowded its stage with such a sumptuous and bespangled revue as cannot possibly earn them anything more substantial than the heart-warming satisfaction of having produced it all.[9]

Although Woollcott may have been dazzled by the sumptuous theater and the spectacular revue, he made one observation that showed why he was regarded as one of the shrewdest of critics. Astutely singling out "Say It with Music," Woollcott called it the "only one real song" in the score and predicted "by February you will have heard it so often that you will gladly shoot at sunrise anyone who so much as hums it in your hearing."[10]

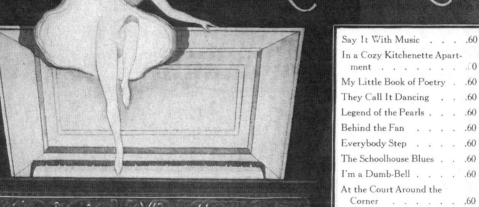

Say It With Music

Words and Music by
IRVING BERLIN

Arranged by
Charles N. Grant

4

So if you have some - thing sweet to tell her:
Just ex - act - ly what I want to tell you:

REFRAIN

Say it with mu - sic, Beau -

p - mf
dolce e legato

ti - ful mu - sic; Some - how they'd

mf - f molto marc.

rath - er be kissed ___ To the strains of Cho - pin or Liszt.

marc.

Say It With Music. 3

219

With all of his success as a songwriter, publisher, and producer, Berlin was ready to dispense advice about the craft of writing songs. In a 1920 interview with the *American Magazine*, he laid out "Nine Rules for Writing Songs," as if anyone could produce the brilliant work he had by following a few simple formulas. Still, the list, as summarized by his biographer Laurence Bergreen, reveals his working methods:

1. The melody should be within the range of most singers.
2. The title should be attention-getting and, in addition, repeated within the body of the song.
3. The song should be "sexless": able to be sung by men and women.
4. The song requires "heart interest."
5. And at the same time, it should be "original in idea, words, and music."
6. "Stick to nature. . . . Not nature in a visionary, abstract way, but nature as demonstrated in homely, concrete, everyday manifestations."
7. Sprinkle the lyrics with "open vowels" so that it will be euphonious.
8. Make the song as simple as possible.
9. "The songwriter must look upon his work as a business, that is, to make a success of it, he must work and work and then WORK."[11]

Berlin might have added a tenth rule: Be alert to shifting cultural appetites and tastes—something he had done throughout his career and did again in the early 1920s when he began writing what he called his "sob ballads"—slow, sad songs that spoke to a collective sense of solitude among urban dwellers. This sense of loneliness was especially poignant among young women, many of whom had come from small towns to find jobs in big-city offices, shops, and the new "department stores." With a freedom unheard of a generation before, they lived on their own in apartments and pursued their recreation unchaperoned. The new convenience of "canned" food and laundromats made single life easier, but there was still an emptiness that T. S. Eliot captured in *The Waste Land* (1922). In his portrait of a young typist who invites a clerk to her flat for dinner, they eat "food in tins," then he engages her in "caresses" that are "unreproved if undesired." Capitulating in "indifference," she accepts a "final patronizing kiss" from her departing lover:

> *When lovely woman stoops to folly and*
> *Paces about her room again, alone,*
> *She smoothes her hair with automatic hand,*
> *And puts a record on the gramophone.*

The record that Eliot's typist puts on her gramophone could easily have been one of Berlin's sob ballads.

Such ballads found their audiences through phonograph records rather than sheet music. Records had been part of the music business since the turn of the century, but they had always been regarded by Tin Pan Alley as a sideline to the sales of sheet music. In 1910, music publishers had succeeded in getting a copyright law passed that required record companies to pay a few cents to music publishers, composers, and lyricists from sales of phonograph records and piano rolls.

Still, to veterans of the music business like Irving Berlin, phonograph records represented a falling away from their mission to supply songs for the public to perform. In the course of his lifetime, Berlin witnessed a shift in popular culture from performance to consumption, in everything from songs to sports. Tin Pan Alley firms marketed sheet music to people who played it on pianos in their own homes. With the development of the player piano, however, one need not play at all, and Tin Pan Alley began to supplement sheet-music sales with player piano "rolls" that were cut by professional performers like George Gershwin and then purchased for reproduction at home. With the increasing popularity of the player piano and the phonograph, people simply listened to songs rather than play them. Indicative of this shift, "All by Myself," one of Berlin's first sob ballads, sold 161,650 piano rolls, 1,053,493 copies of sheet music, and 1,225,083 phonograph records.

At this same time, another technological innovation transformed the music business. On November 2, 1920, the first radio station, KDKA in Pittsburgh, broadcast the election returns that made Warren Gamaliel Harding the twenty-ninth president of the United States. Radio was slow to catch on, however, as stations tried broadcasting church services, concerts, and even the boxing match between Jack Dempsey and Georges Carpentier. When they began playing popular songs, however, the entire country perked up its ears. "There is radio music in the air, every night, everywhere," newspapers announced. "Anybody can hear it at home on a receiving set, which any boy can put up in an hour."[12]

President Harding had a radio installed in the White House. Radio sales hit $60 million in 1922, doubled in 1923, nearly tripled in 1924, then reached half a billion dollars in 1925.

Now, ASCAP insisted that radio stations, like restaurants and cabarets before them, had to purchase a license to play the songs of Irving Berlin, Jerome Kern, and other ASCAP members. At first stations argued, as restaurants and cabarets had done, that songwriters should be grateful to radio for plugging their songs, but radio too had to come around. When every radio station had to buy an annual license, ASCAP revenues swelled.

Radio was the ultimate "plugger" of a new song, and Berlin shrewdly realized that it called for his sob ballads—intimate and introspective—aimed at the solitary listener rather than a theater audience or a group sing-a-long around the parlor piano. "All by Myself," was the number one song for seven weeks in the fall of 1921. It was followed by "All Alone" (1924) "What'll I Do?" (1924), and "Always" (1925), some of which were introduced on radio. Berlin's sob ballads spoke to their listeners in their pensive moments as did his rhythmic songs in their lively ones.

ALL BY MYSELF

By Irving Berlin

Irving Berlin Inc.
MUSIC PUBLISHERS
1587 Broadway   New York

All By Myself

Words and Music by
IRVING BERLIN

Moderato

I'm so un-hap - py

My name and num - ber

What - 'll I do, ___ I long for some - bo - dy who, ___

are in the book, ___ The one that hangs on a hook, ___

will sym - pa - thize with me; I'm grow - ing so tired of

In al - most ev - 'ry drug store; Why don't ___ some - one

All By Myself - 3

226

Gus Kahn

GUSTAV GERSON KAHN was born in 1886 in Koblenz, Germany, but his family emigrated in 1891, when Kahn was only four, and settled in Chicago. He dropped out of school to work at various jobs, but he also wrote lyrics and comic sketches for vaudeville. He wrote several songs with composer Grace LeBoy, and the two collaborators married in 1915. In that same year, the established Tin Pan Alley composer Egbert Van Alstyne turned to Kahn when his longtime lyricist, Harry Williams, moved to the West Coast. In 1915, Kahn had his first hit with Van Alstyne, "Memories," then in 1916 they followed with "Pretty Baby." By the 1920s, Kahn had mastered the craft of setting vernacular lyrics to the jazzy music of the new decade.

In 1921, given the repeated four-note musical phrases of composer Richard Whiting, Kahn, with co-lyricist Raymond Egan, hit his vernacular stride with "Ain't We Got Fun":

Ev'ry morning, ev'ry evening, ain't we got fun?
Not much money, oh, but honey, ain't we got fun?

Not only do Kahn and Egan use abrupt, colloquial—even ungrammatical—phrases, they abandon syntax for the telegraphic connections of conversation. Truncated slang phrases such as "Not much money" are the verbal equivalent of the syncopated musical fragments, and Kahn and Egan heighten the ragged feel of both music and words with rhymes that come off and on the beat—*got* against *not, fun* against *mon*-ey and *hon*-ey. The playfulness of both music and lyric drops a proverbial rhyme in a winking celebration of the sexual compensations of poverty:

There's nothing sure-
er:

The rich get rich and the poor
Get children.

Kahn and Egan also use alliteration to underscore their innuendoes, the *ch* of ri*ch* begetting *ch*ildren, though rhyme can also cleverly serve their suggestive ends:

In the mean *time,*
*In bet*ween *time,*
Ain't we got fun?

The repetitiveness of musical and lyrical phrasing suggest the incessantly frenetic "fun" itself. It's not surprising that F. Scott Fitzgerald has Jay Gatsby nervously request this song to celebrate his reunion with Daisy Buchanan in *The Great Gatsby.*

"Ain't We Got Fun" was initially popularized by the tenor-baritone duo of Gus Van and Joe Schenck, who laced their singing act with dialect sketches. The song was in the Top Ten from May through December 1921 and was the number one song for three weeks in June of that year.

Although New York was the hub of popular music, Kahn remained in Chicago with his family. There, as Kahn's son Donald said, "He spent half of his time on the golf course and the other half in nightclubs, where he was known as the 'King of Chicago.'"[1] He would sometimes travel to New York to work on songs with composers, but more frequently New York composers would travel to Chicago for the privilege of collaborating with Gus Kahn. These collaborations produced some of the most memorable hits of the Roaring Twenties, such as Kahn's lyric to a melody by Ernie Erdman, Ted Fiorito, and Robert A. King, "Toot, Toot, Tootsie! (Good-bye)," which Al Jolson sang in *Bombo* (1921). It turned into one of the biggest hits of the decade.

Over the course of his career, Gus Kahn wrote more than two thousand lyrics and, for twenty years, had an average of six hit songs a year. He worked at lyric writing incessantly, sometimes stopping a golf game to jot down ideas on his scorecard or pausing at dinner to write lyrics on his napkin.

AIN'T WE GOT FUN
SONG

Lyric by
GUS KAHN
& RAYMOND B. EGAN

Music by
RICHARD A. WHITING

Moderato

Bill col - lec - tors gath - er 'Round and rath - er
Just to make their troub - le Near - ly doub - le

Haunt the cot - tage next door Men the gro - cer and
Some - thing hap - pen'd last night To their chim - ney a

2221-4

butch - er sent / gray bird came — Men who call for the / Mis - ter Stork is his — rent / name — But with - / And I'll

\- in a hap - py / bet two pins — A — chap - py And his / pair of twins Just — bride of on - ly a / hap - pen'd in with the

year — / bird — Seem to be so cheer - ful / Still they're ver - y — Here's an ear full / gay and mer - ry

Of the chat - ter you / Just at dawn - ing I — hear / heard

Ain't We Got Fun - 4

3

Ain't We Got Fun - 4

In the win-ter in the sum-mer Don't we have fun
Land-lords mad and get-ting mad-der Ain't we got fun

Times are bum and get-ting bum-mer Still we have fun
Times are bad and get-ting bad-der Still we have fun

cresc.

There's noth-ing sur — er The rich get rich and the poor get chil-dren
There's noth-ing sur — er The rich get rich and the poor get laid off

cresc.

1.
In the mean-time In be-tween time Ain't we got fun
In the mean-time In be-tween time Ain't we got

2.
D.C.
fun

D.C.

Ain't We Got Fun -4

Walter Donaldson

IN 1922, GUS KAHN began collaborating with Walter Donaldson, who was born in Brooklyn on February 15, 1893. His mother was a piano teacher who nurtured the musical talents of her eleven children. Walter started as a piano plugger, demonstrating songs in five-and-dime stores to boost sheet-music sales. He also accompanied silent movies in nickelodeons. Donaldson broke into Tin Pan Alley as a staff pianist but soon began writing his own songs. After he served in World War I, Donaldson had his first big hit with "How Ya Gonna Keep 'Em Down on the Farm (After They've Seen Paree)?" which James Reese Europe and his African-American jazz band introduced in a New York victory parade after the armistice in 1918.

Gus Kahn and Walter Donaldson would write more than a hundred songs together, many of them hits, and some became enduring standards. Like Kahn, Donaldson worked incessantly. Both were avid golfers and frequently worked as they played on the course. One of their first big hits was "My Buddy" (1922), which Donaldson wrote as an expression of grief over the death of his fiancée but which Americans embraced as a lament for all the "buddies" lost during World War I.

In the same year, they wrote an even more enduring song, "Carolina in the Morning." Donaldson's music carried the repetitive style of the 1920s to an extreme. He frequently built his melodies around the insistent device of moving back and forth between just two notes, which he did in "My Buddy" and did again in "Carolina in the Morning." Alec Wilder, who usually disliked such repetitive melodies, observed, "Granted, it's monotonous, yet its very insistence was what caught the public's fancy." What delighted Wilder, however, was this "unexpected caper" near the end of the melody, which Kahn set with clever internal rhymes:

If I had A-lad-din's lamp for only a day

Wilder found the phrase "unexpectedly inventive, specifically the drop to low *c*" on "day."[1]

Elsewhere in the song, Kahn emphasized the to-and-fro pattern of Donaldson's music with more internal rhymes:

> *Where the* mor-*ning* glor-*ies*
> *Twine around the* door,
> *Whispering pretty* stor-*ies*
> *I long to hear once* more.

Still, Kahn could also sidestep monotony with an occasional off-rhyme: "Nothing could be *finer* than to be in Caro*lina.*"

"Carolina in the Morning" was the number one song for five weeks in early 1923, followed closely by "My Buddy."

CAROLINA IN THE MORNING
SONG

Lyric by
GUS KAHN

Music by
WALTER DONALDSON

VOICE

PIANO

Wish - ing is good - time wast - ed Still it's a hab - it they say
Dream - ing was meant for night-time I live in dreams all the day

Wish - ing for sweets I've tast - ed That's all I do — all day
I know it's not the right time But still I dream a - way

Carolina In The Morning-4

But - ter - flies all flut - ter up and kiss each lit - tle but - ter - cup at dawn -

-ing   If I had A - lad - din's lamp for   on - ly a   day —

I'd   make a wish and here's what I'd say —   Noth - ing could be fin - er than to

be in Car - o - lin - a in the   morn - - ing - - ing

fz   D.C.

Fred Fisher

FRED FISHER WAS BORN Albert von Breitenbach in Cologne, Germany, in 1875. At age thirteen he ran away from home and joined the German navy. A few years later, he enlisted in the French Foreign Legion. In 1900, he came to the United States and settled in Chicago, where a black saloon musician taught him how to play the piano. Soon he changed his name to Friedrich Fischer— "Friedrich" for its Teutonic strength and "Fischer"—with a "c"—from a sign he read on a passing truck. He began writing songs, such as "Come, Josephine, in My Flying Machine" (1910). He also wrote "Peg O' My Heart" (1913) and so many other Irish songs that he earned a place in *The Guinness Book of World Records* for Irish songs.

With the onset of World War I, he thought Friedrich Fischer sounded *too* Germanic, so he took the "c" out of Fischer and shortened his first name to Fred. He never lost his German accent. Fisher was capable of bizarre behavior. He once asked a visitor to his office if he wanted to see something funny. Fisher then picked up a typewriter and threw it out the window; it landed on the sidewalk— luckily not on any pedestrians—many stories below.

Fisher usually wrote songs in collaboration with a lyricist, but for his most enduring song, "Chicago," he wrote both music and lyrics. He captured much of the energy of the "toddling town" he knew so well in the Roaring Twenties and included such period allusions as "Billy Sunday." Billy Sunday was a baseball player turned evangelist, who would perform athletic stunts, such as sliding into second base for Jesus, as part of his revival meetings. An ardent Prohibitionist, Sunday vowed to make America so dry you'd have to prime a man before he could spit. He devoted himself to shutting down saloons, sometimes every saloon in town.

But not in Chicago—"the town that Billy Sunday could not shut down."

"CHICAGO"
That Toddling Town

By FRED FISHER

243

ad lib

clare, You're not a ware, Just where to go, _____ When you're in
band, Right here on hand, or else their cheap, _____ If you'll in-

town, Just call a-round, right there I'm found, Real-ly you ought to know: _____
-vest, You'll find a guest, they'll nev-er rest, They're danc-ing while they sleep: _____

Chorus

Chi-ca-go,___ Chi-ca-go,___ That tod-dle-ing town, Tod-dl'-ing Town, Chi-

-ca-go,___ Chi-ca-go,___ I'll show you a-round,___ I love it,

Chicago 4

244

4

Betch your bot-tom dol-lar you lose the blues — in Chi - ca - go, — Chi - ca - go, — The

town that Bill - y Sun-day could not — shut down, —————— On

State Street, That Great Street, — I just want to say, — Just want to say, — They

do things — they dont do on Broad-way, Say,

They have the time, The time — of their life, I saw a man he danced with his wife, in Chi-

Ira Gershwin

WHEN THEY WERE KIDS, Ira was always more successful than his younger brother, but when George quit school to pursue a musical career, their fortunes reversed. George wrote several hit songs and by 1920 was writing scores for Broadway musicals. Ira had to drop out of City College of New York when he couldn't pass mathematics and wound up in several odd jobs, including handing out towels at his father's bathhouse. While he sat at the bathhouse desk, he would write light-verse poems and comic sketches.

He showed some of his writing to one of the residents who lived above the bathhouse—Paul M. Potter, the English playwright who had dramatized George du Maurier's best-selling novel *Trilby*. Potter gave Ira some sound advice. First, he said, "Learn especially your American slang."[1] Englishman that he was, Potter recognized that the American vernacular was a far richer idiom than the stilted language Ira was using.

Potter's second piece of advice implied that Ira's shyness and reticence—compared to his brother's flamboyance—might actually be an asset in a literary life: he seemed to think that "a writer doesn't necessarily have to experience everything he writes about, but by being an attentive listener and observer, can gain a good deal by second hand experience."[2]

Finally, Potter suggested that Ira send one of his sketches to H. L. Mencken and George Jean Nathan's *Smart Set*, the most sophisticated magazine of the day. Mencken promptly sent Ira a letter of acceptance, a request for more submissions, and a check—for one dollar. Buddy DeSylva, who at the time was collaborating with George Gershwin, told Ira that he would "have preferred getting a dollar check from Mencken than several thousands from Remick's." "This was very charming," Ira observed, "but the fact remains" that DeSylva "died leaving several millions."[3]

The irony of "Ira, the Scholar," out of school and adrift, while his younger brother, who once seemed destined for nothing but trouble, rose to success, was not lost upon Ira. "I now belong, I see," he wrote to a friend, thanking him for newspaper clippings about George, "to the ranks of Brothers of the Great."[4] When George was hired by Max Dreyfus at T. B. Harms, Ira recorded the event in his diary with pride but also a tinge of envy:

> George has been placed on the staff of T. B. Harms Co. He gets $35 a week for this connection, then $50 advance and a 3 cents royalty on each song of his they accept. This entails no other effort on his part than the composing, they not requiring any of his leisure for plugging nor for piano-playing. Some snap.[5]

Ira described his own situation in much gloomier terms:

> I'm afraid I was pretty much of a floating soul. I couldn't concentrate on anything....To tell the truth, I was at a complete loss and I didn't care. It was at this moment that I first thought of becoming a writer of what they call "lyrics."[6]

As a sign of his determination to become a lyricist, he purchased a rhyming dictionary and *Roget's Thesaurus*.

Ira pursued his new career in between passing out towels at the bathhouse, and finally, on bathhouse stationery under the imprint "ST. NICHOLAS BATHS, Russian and Turkish," wrote a lyric, "The Great American Folk Song (Is a Rag)," and presented it to his brother.

"Geo. Liked it," Ira recorded in his diary. George, with his usual flair, proceeded to dash off some music to fit Ira's words:

> So we sat down on, (at, rather) the piano & Geo. started something. Something sounded good so we kept it. It was a strain for the first two lines. That in our possession we went along legitimate or illegitimate (if you prefer) rag lines and with a little editing here & there the chorus, musical, stood forth in all its glory.

At that point, however, Ira's lyrical apprenticeship began in earnest, for he realized that George's melody did not fit his words.

> … unhappily, the musical lines were of different lengths from the lyric, so after having sweated & toiled & moiled over 20 or so different versions, it now devolves upon me to start an entirely new one.[7]

Although Ira had written his lyric first, he was now learning that in American popular song, it was the music that had primacy, and he would have to find syllables, words, and phrases that matched, mosaically, his brother's musical notes.

His words would also have to flow more "singably," so that the title of the song changed from the guttural and dental consonants of "Great" to the fricative and liquid consonants of "Real."

While "The Real American Folk Song" was not a hit, it provided Ira Gershwin his first lesson in writing "what they call 'lyrics.'" Years later, he would reflect, "It takes years and years of experience to know that such a note cannot take such a syllable, that many a poetic line can be unsingable, that many an ordinary line fitted into the proper musical phrase can sound like a million."[8] "Good lyrics," he told an interviewer, "should be simple, colloquial, rhymed conversational phrases." He told another, "he had tried 'to capture the ways people spoke to each other—their slang, their clichés, their catchphrases.'"[9]

He learned those lessons by working with George as well as with other composers. To make sure no one could accuse him of riding on his brother's coattails, he wrote under a pseudonym—"Arthur Francis"—a pen name derived from the names of his other brother and his sister Frances. While his fifty or so lyrics written between 1918 and 1922 were solid apprentice work, only one was commercially successful. In 1921, he was working with composer Vincent Youmans on songs for the musical *Two Little Girls in Blue*. One of Youmans's melodies consisted of a series of three two-note drops. Ira matched the first two drops with two ordinary exclamations:

Oh me!
Oh my!

But for the third drop Ira gave rein to his playfulness with American slang, enlivening the clichéd "Oh me! Oh my!" by throwing in the skewedly parallel:

Oh you!

This engaging series of phrases was initially a "dummy lyric," a temporary lyric that Ira, like most lyricists who could not read music, used to help him remember a melody while he worked on the "real" lyric. Youmans, however, urged him to make the dummy lyric the real one because it was a perfect fit between verbal and musical accents. The lyric was also eminently "singable" as it oscillated between long open and closed vowels—*o*h and m*e*, *o*h and m*y*—then culminated in the two long, open vowels of *o*h and *you*. At Youmans's urging, Ira agreed to using the dummy lyric, "which was fine with me," he recalled later with characteristic modesty, "because I couldn't think of anything else."[10] A few years later, Youmans would urge another collaborator, Irving Caesar, to use a dummy lyric as the real lyric for a song that would become their biggest hit—"Tea for Two."

Since 1920 George Gershwin had been writing songs for *George White's Scandals*, a series of annual revues, similar to *Ziegfeld's Follies*, that featured songs, dances, comedy routines, and scantily clad women. For the 1922 edition, lyricist Buddy DeSylva asked Ira about a song he had written with George back in 1919,

"A New Step Every Day." DeSylva said he thought the last line of the song—"I'll build a staircase to paradise with a new step ev'ry day"—could be the basis of a production number. Perhaps thinking of Ziegfeld's use of a staircase to display a bevy of chorines, DeSylva told Ira "If you like, we could write it up and I *think* it could be used in the *Scandals*."[11]

"Naturally I was tickled to be able to collaborate on something for the *Scandals*," Ira recalled but thought George's melody, "replete with sixteenth notes and thick chords, plus a refrain with key changes," would keep the song from becoming popular.[12] Still, he and DeSylva went to work on the lyric at DeSylva's Greenwich Village apartment at nine that evening and finished the song at two the next morning. Except for the last line of "A New Step Every Day," their lyric was completely new, and probably DeSylva's more experienced ear suggested "staircase" be changed to the more "singable" "stair*way*."

Although he was pleased to have a song in the *Scandals*, Ira was sure "my returns would be program credit and nothing else."[13] Therefore he was pleasantly surprised when the song was one of seven from the show selected for sheet-music publication. "The bands around town and some record companies played up "Stairway to Paradise" more than anything else in the show, and it became a hit— that is, for a revue."[14] (Most hit songs from the stage, Ira explained, emerge from "book" musicals rather than revues.)

Equally gratifying was the money he earned from the song. "My one-third of 'Stairway's royalties amounted to thirty-five hundred dollars, enough to support me for the year."[15] On the strength of that success, he dropped the pseudonym "Arthur Francis" and began placing "Ira Gershwin" on the sheet music for his songs. Many years later, however, he would cast a critical eye on the first lines of the verse of his journeyman effort:

> *All you preachers,*
> *Who delight in panning the dancing teachers,*
> *Let me tell you there are a lot of features*
> *Of the dance that carry you through*
> *The Gates of Heaven.*

Although one of his many rhyming dictionaries listed "feature" as a rhyme for "teacher," the master craftsman would observe, "I doubt that I'd rhyme them today."[16]

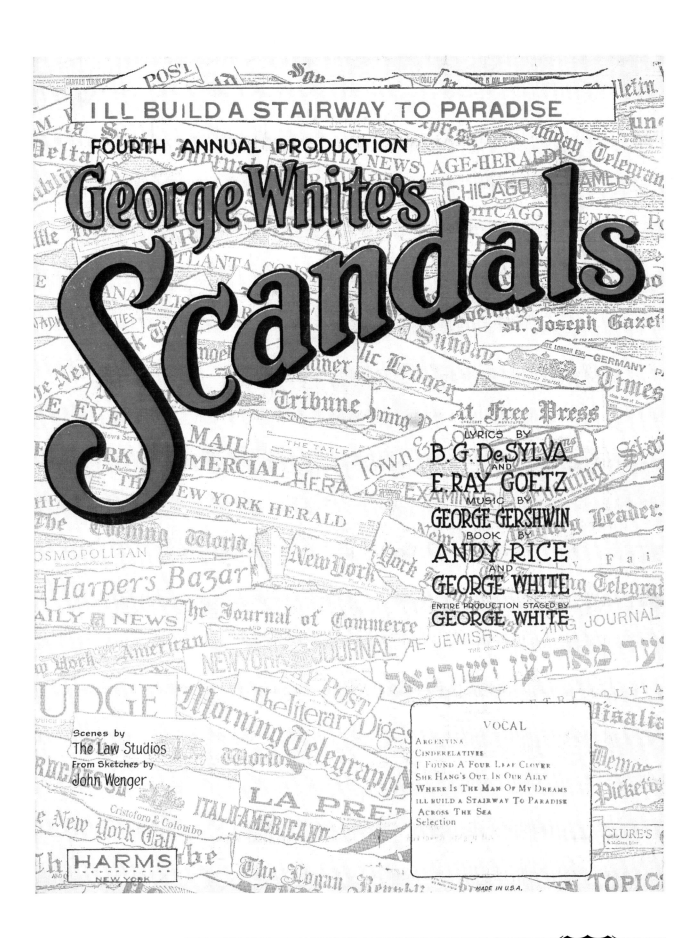

2

I'll Build A
Stairway To Paradise

Words by
B. G. DE SYLVA and
ARTHUR FRANCIS

Music by
GEORGE GERSHWIN

4

find it nice   The quick-est way   to   Par - a - dise

When you prac-tise   Here's the thing to do   Sim-ply say as you go. ___

Refrain *Con spirito*

I'll build a stair-way to   Par-a-dise With a   new step ev-'ry

day!   I'm going to get there at   a-ny price Stand a-

6544_4 Stairway To Paradise

George Gershwin would write songs for two more annual editions of *George White's Scandals*; by 1924, both he and Ira would begin writing almost exclusively for Broadway musicals, having their first major success that year with *Lady, Be Good!* which heralded a change in American popular music. Increasingly, popular songs would emerge from Broadway shows rather than the cubicles of Tin Pan Alley sheet-music publishing offices. Writing songs for Broadway, Ira Gershwin realized, gave songs "particularity," for they were what he called "lodgments" for specific characters to sing at certain dramatic moments as opposed to the generic warbles of "me" to "you" in Tin Pan Alley fare. Just as he was injecting more character and drama into songs, his brother George was infusing Broadway music with jazz and blues. In the wings were other young songwriters, such as Lorenz Hart and Richard Rodgers, Cole Porter, and Harold Arlen, who would bring American popular song into the Jazz Age. These Broadway songwriters would soon displace the lyricists and composers of Tin Pan Alley.

The demise of Tin Pan Alley was hastened by the development of talking pictures in the late 1920s. Tin Pan Alley had long used films as a place to plug its wares, from song slides in storefront nickelodeons to "theme" or "title" songs for silent movies. But with the advent of sound, Hollywood studios needed songs and began buying out the sheet-music publishers of Tin Pan Alley. Warner Bros., the first studio to present talking pictures, bought out the publishing houses of Witmark and Son, T. B. Harms, and Remick. Other studios did the same, moving songwriters out of their cubicles on Tin Pan Alley and onto studio lots, where they were told to "write hits" for the movies. The role of the Tin Pan Alley sheet-music publisher as one who sought out ideas for new songs, supervised the assembly-line production of songs, and then disseminated songs through a network of pluggers was coming to an end. "All we do," one publisher lamented, "is collect royalties."[17]

Notes and References

Introduction

1. E. Y. Harburg, "From the Lower East Side to 'Over the Rainbow,'" in *Creators and Disturbers: Reminiscences by Jewish Intellectuals of New York*, ed. Bernard Rosenberg and Ernest Goldstein (New York: Columbia University Press, 1982), 140–41.
2. Larry Stempel, *Showtime: A History of the Broadway Musical Theater* (New York: W. W. Norton, 2010), 249.
3. *AARP: The Magazine*, February/March 2015, 28.

Tin Pan Alley

1. Warren Craig, *Sweet and Lowdown: America's Popular Song Writers* (Metuchen, NJ: Scarecrow Press, Inc., 1978), 15.
2. David Ewen, *The Life and Death of Tin Pan Alley: The Golden Age of American Popular Music* (New York: Funk and Wagnalls, 1964), 4–5.
3. David Jasen, *Tin Pan Alley* (New York: Donald I. Fine, Inc., 1988), xvi.
4. Kenneth Aaron Kanter, *The Jews on Tin Pan Alley* (New York: Ktav Publishing House, Inc., 1982), 17.
5. David A. Jasen and Gene Jones, *Spreadin' Rhythm Around: Black Popular Songwriters, 1880–1930* (New York: Schirmer Books, 1998), 17.

Charles K. Harris

1. Charles K. Harris, *After the Ball: Forty Years of Melody* (New York: Frank Maurice, 1926), 62–64.
2. Harris, *After the Ball,* 19.
3. Harris, *After the Ball,* 67.
4. Harris, *After the Ball,* 72.

5. Harris, *After the Ball*, 73.
6. Charles Hamm, *Yesterdays: Popular Song in America* (New York: W. W. Norton, 1979), 292.
7. Harris, *After the Ball*, 2.
8. Harris, *After the Ball*, 9–10.
9. Harris, *After the Ball*, 127–28.
10. Harris, *After the Ball*, 20–21.
11. Harris, *After the Ball*, 176–77.
12. Harris, *After the Ball*, 178–81.
13. Robert Lissauer, *Lissauer's Encyclopedia of Popular Music in America, 1888 to the Present* (New York: Paragon House, 1991), 499.
14. Harris, *After the Ball*, 13.
15. Harris, *After the Ball*, 275–79.
16. Philip Furia, *Skylark: The Life and Times of Johnny Mercer* (New York: St. Martin's Press, 2003), 51–63.

Ragtime

1. Gerald Bordman, *American Musical Comedy: From "Adonis" to "Dream Girls"* (New York: Oxford University Press, 1982), 77.
2. Jasen and Jones, *Spreadin' Rhythm Around*, 32.
3. Jasen and Jones, *Spreadin' Rhythm Around*, 23.
4. Isaac Goldberg, *Tin Pan Alley* (New York: John Day Company, 1930), 230.

Bob Cole and J. Rosamond and James Weldon Johnson

1. Eugene D. Levy, *James Weldon Johnson: Black Leader, Black Voice* (Chicago: University of Chicago Press, 1973), 87–88.
2. Sigmund Spaeth, *A History of Popular Music in America* (New York: Random House, 1948), 338.
3. Jasen and Jones, *Spreadin' Rhythm Around*, 105.
4. Max Morath, "Introduction," *Favorite Songs of the Nineties*, ed. Robert A. Fremont (New York: Dover, 1973), ix.

George M. Cohan

1. Bordman, *American Musical Comedy*, 66–67.
2. Leonard Bernstein, *The Joy of Music* (New York: Simon and Schuster, 1959), 166–67.

Shelton Brooks

1. Jasen and Jones, *Spreadin' Rhythm Around*, 145.
2. Jasen, *Tin Pan Alley*, 87.
3. Sophie Tucker, *Some of These Days* (Garden City, NY: Garden City Publishing Company, 1945), 114.

4. Alec Wilder, *American Popular Song: The Great Innovators, 1900–1950* (New York: Oxford University Press, 1972), 14.

5. For the "chart" figures for "Some of These Days" and other songs, we are indebted to Edward Foote Garner's meticulous study, *Popular Songs of the Twentieth Century: A Charted History,* vol. 1, *Chart Detail & Encyclopedia, 1900–1949* (St. Paul, MN: Paragon House, 2000).

Irving Berlin

1. Charles Hamm, *Irving Berlin: Songs from the Melting Pot: The Formative Years, 1907–1914* (New York: Oxford University Press, 1997), 115.

2. Philip Furia, *Irving Berlin: A Life in Song* (New York: Schirmer Books, 1998), 38.

3. Furia, *Berlin: Life in Song,* 39. Citing the copyright entry cards in the Library of Congress, Charles Hamm has noted that the song with "words and music by Irving Berlin" was registered for copyright in March 1911, while an instrumental "march and two-step" was registered in September of that year. Hamm concludes, despite Berlin's own assertion, that "Alexander's Ragtime Band" was not originally an instrumental but a *song* with both music and a lyric. The instrumental came later. (Hamm, *Berlin: Songs*), 112.

4. Furia, *Berlin: Life in Song,* 25. The cover of the sheet music has a misspelling: "Successfully Intruduced by Emma Carus."

The Dance Craze

1. Lewis Erenberg, *Steppin' Out: New York Nightlife and the Transformation of American Culture, 1890–1930* (Westport, CT: Greenwood Press, 1981), 81.

2. Erenberg, *Steppin' Out,* 146.

3. Erenberg, *Steppin' Out,* 116.

4. Edgar A. Berlin, *Reflections and Research on Ragtime* (Brooklyn, NY: Institute for Studies in American Music, 1987), 67.

5. Erenberg, *Steppin' Out,* 155.

6. Erenberg, *Steppin' Out,* 81.

7. Furia, *Berlin: Life in Song,* 51.

8. Mark Grant, *The Rise and Fall of the Broadway Musical* (Boston: Northeastern University Press, 2004), 136.

9. Jasen and Jones, *Spreadin' Rhythm Around,* 162. Jasen and Jones also note, "The dance also had other claimants besides the Castles. One of these was the black pianist Hughie Woolford, who said that his playing at the Trouville Restaurant on Long Island inspired the trotting of the vaudeville dancer Harry Fox, who created the classic step."

10. Furia, *Berlin: Life in Song,* 52.

11. Edgar Berlin, *Reflections and Research,* 69.

12. Furia, *Berlin: Life in Song,* 52.

13. Furia, *Berlin: Life in Song,* 53. On the sheet music cover, as well as in the lyric, the title of the song is printed as "Everybody's Doin' It," but on the first page of the music itself the title is the more proper "Everybody's Doing It."

Ernie Burnett

1. Wilder, *American Popular Song,* 17.

W. C. Handy

1. W. C. Handy, *Father of the Blues,* ed. Arna Bontemps (New York: Macmillan, 1947), 9.
2. Jasen and Jones, *Spreadin' Rhythm Around,* 224.
3. Handy, *Father of the Blues,* 10.
4. Handy, *Father of the Blues,* 34.
5. Handy, *Father of the Blues,* 75.
6. Handy, *Father of the Blues,* 93–94.
7. Handy, *Father of the Blues,* 108.
8. Handy, *Father of the Blues,* 119.
9. Handy, *Father of the Blues,* 121.
10. Handy, *Father of the Blues,* 120.
11. Handy, *Father of the Blues,* 122.

Jerome Kern

1. Lee Davis, *Bolton and Wodehouse and Kern: The Men Who Made Musical Comedy* (New York: James H. Heineman, Inc., 1993), 35.
2. Wilder, *American Popular Song,* 34–35.
3. Bordman, *American Musical Comedy,* 103.

ASCAP

1. Ewen, *Tin Pan Alley,* 209–13.

Irving Berlin on Broadway

1. Furia, *Berlin*: *Life in Song,*, 59.
2. Stempel, *Showtime,* 154.
3. Furia, *Berlin*: *Life in Song,* 60.
4. Furia, *Berlin*: *Life in Song,* 64.
5. Furia, *Berlin*: *Life in Song,* 64.
6. Stempel, *Showtime,* 154.
7. Harry Smith, *First Nights and First Editions* (Boston: Little Brown, 1931), 282.
8. Furia, *Berlin*: *Life in Song,* 34.
9. Wilder, *American Popular Song,* 98.

Spencer Williams

1. Jasen and Jones, *Spreadin' Rhythm Around,* 169.
2. Jasen and Jones, *Spreadin' Rhythm Around,* 170.
3. Jasen and Jones, *Spreadin' Rhythm Around,* 170.

George M. Cohan Goes to War

1. Philip Furia and Michael Lasser, *America's Songs: The Stories Behind the Songs of Broadway, Hollywood, and Tin Pan Alley* (New York: Routledge, 2006), 18.

The Princess Shows

1. Davis, *Men Who Made Musical Comedy,* ix. As Lee Davis notes, this poem was probably written by George S. Kaufman.
2. Bordman, *American Musical Comedy,* 94.
3. Davis, *Men Who Made Musical Comedy,* 69.
4. Bordman, *American Musical Comedy,* 76.
5. Davis, *Men Who Made Musical Comedy,* 71.
6. Davis, *Men Who Made Musical Comedy,* 121.
7. Stempel, *Showtime,* 169.
8. Bordman, *American Musical Comedy,* 100.

P. G. Wodehouse

1. Davis, *Men Who Made Musical Comedy,* 87.
2. Davis, *Men Who Made Musical Comedy,* 116.
3. P. G. Wodehouse, *Author! Author!* (New York: Simon and Schuster, 1962), 15.
4. Davis, *Men Who Made Musical Comedy,* 123.
5. Davis, *Men Who Made Musical Comedy,* 109.
6. Samuel Marx and Jan Clayton, *Rodgers and Hart* (New York: G. P. Putnam's Sons, 1976), 38.
7. Deena Rosenberg, *Fascinating Rhythm: The Collaboration of George and Ira Gershwin* (New York: Dutton, 1991), 397.

Henry Creamer and Turner Layton

1. Jasen and Jones, *Spreadin' Rhythm Around,* 365.

Joseph McCarthy and Harry Carroll

1. Furia and Lasser, *America's Songs,* 24.

Private Irving Berlin

1. Furia, *Berlin: Life in Song*, 79.
2. Max Wilk, *They're Playing Our Song* (New York: Atheneum, 1973), 275.
3. Wilk, *Playing Our Song*, 275.

The *Ziegfeld Follies*

1. Bordman, *American Musical Comedy*, 132.
2. Jasen and Jones, *Spreadin' Rhythm Around*, 63.
3. Wilder, *American Popular Song*, 99.
4. Furia, *Berlin: Life in Song*, 86.
5. Furia, *Berlin: Life in Song*, 86.

George Gershwin

1. Edward Jablonski, *Gershwin* (Boston: Northeastern University Press, 1987), 35–36.
2. Jablonski, *Gershwin*, 36.
3. Jablonski, *Gershwin*, 36.
4. Furia and Lasser, *America's Songs*, 26.
5. Furia and Lasser, *America's Songs*, 26.
6. Bordman, *American Musical Comedy*, 123.

Otto Harbach

1. Thomas J. Hischak, "Otto Harbach," *Dictionary of Literary Biography*, vol. 265, *American Song Lyricists, 1920–1960*, ed. Philip Furia (Detroit: Gale, 2002), 211.
2. Bordman, *American Musical Comedy*, 107–8.

Buddy DeSylva

1. DeSylva's name does not appear on the sheet music for "Avalon." The omission may indicate that as a new staff lyricist at Remick's, he was given a flat fee for his lyric and was entitled to no royalties from sheet-music sales. Or the Puccini suit may have prompted him to have his name removed as the lyricist. In later editions of sheet music for "Avalon," he is credited as the lyricist.
2. Furia and Lasser, *America's Songs*, 32.
3. Gerald Bordman, *Jerome Kern: His Life and Music* (New York: Oxford University Press, 1980), 209.

Noble Sissle and Eubie Blake

1. Robert Kimball and William Bolcom, *Reminiscing with Noble Sissle and Eubie Blake* (New York: Cooper Square Press, 2000), 106.

2. Kimball and Bolcom, *Reminiscing,* 106.
3. Kimball and Bolcom, *Reminiscing,* 93.
4. Kimball and Bolcom, *Reminiscing,* 13.
5. Kimball and Bolcom, *Reminiscing,* 93.
6. Jasen and Jones, *Spreadin' Rhythm Around,* 348.

Irving Berlin and the Music Box Theatre

1. Furia, *Berlin: Life in Song,* 87.
2. Alexander Woollcott, *The Story of Irving Berlin* (New York: G. P. Putnam's Sons, 1925), 173–74.
3. Furia, *Berlin: Life in Song,* 88.
4. Michael Freedland, *Irving Berlin* (New York: Stein and Day, 1974), 64–65.
5. Laurence Bergreen, *As Thousands Cheer: The Life of Irving Berlin* (New York: Penguin Books, 1990), 179.
6. Bergreen, *As Thousands Cheer,* 181.
7. Furia, Berlin: *Life in Song,* 87.
8. Freedland, *Irving Berlin,* 69.
9. Furia, *Berlin: Life in Song,* 92.
10. Furia, *Berlin: Life in Song,* 92.
11. Bergreen, *As Thousands Cheer,* 167–68.
12. Frederick Lewis Allen, *Only Yesterday: An Informal History of the 1920s* (New York: Harper and Row, 1931), 65.

Gus Kahn

1. Marty Minchin, "Gus Kahn," *Dictionary of Literary Biography,* vol. 265, 285.

Walter Donaldson

1. Wilder, *American Popular Song,* 389.

Ira Gershwin

1. Philip Furia, *Ira Gershwin: The Art of the Lyricist* (New York: Oxford University Press, 1996), 24.
2. Rosenberg, *Fascinating Rhythm,* 20.
3. David Ewen, *George Gershwin: His Journey to Greatness* (New York: Ungar, 1970), 38–39.
4. S. N. Berman, *People in a Diary* (Boston: Little Brown, 1972), 242.
5. Robert Kimball, *The Complete Lyrics of Ira Gershwin* (New York: Alfred A. Knopf, 1993), 4.
6. Robert Kimball and Alfred Simon, *The Gershwins* (New York: Atheneum, 1973), xxii.
7. Rosenberg, *Fascinating Rhythm,* 33.
8. Ira Gershwin, *Lyrics on Several Occasions* (New York: Alfred A. Knopf, 1959), 360.

9. Kimball, *Complete Lyrics,* xvi.

10. Furia, *Ira Gershwin,* 36.

11. Ira Gershwin, *Lyrics,* 295.

12. Ira Gershwin, *Lyrics,* 295.

13. Ira Gershwin, *Lyrics,* 295.

14. Ira Gershwin, *Lyrics,* 296.

15. Ira Gershwin, *Lyrics,* 296.

16. Ira Gershwin, *Lyrics,* 296.

17. Gerald Mast, *The American Musical on Stage and Screen* (Woodstock, NY: Overlook Press, 1987), 124.